The News-Gazette

FIGHTING ILLINI BASKETBALL

A HARDWOOD HISTORY

Published by Sports Publishing Inc.
www.News-Gazettebooks.com

FIGHTING ILLINI BASKETBALL
A HARDWOOD HISTORY

The News-Gazette®

MARAJEN STEVICK CHINIGO, Publisher

JEFF D' ALESSIO AND JIM ROSSOW, Coordinating Editors

JOANNA WRIGHT, Acquisitions Editor

SUSAN M. MCKINNEY, Director of Production

JENNIFER L. POLSON, Interior Design, Senior Project Manager

TERRY NEUTZ HAYDEN, Dustjacket and Insert Design

ISBN 1-58261-273-0

Published by Sports Publishing Inc.

www.News-Gazettebooks.com

CONTENTS

FOREWORD

BY LOREN TATE

I t was start-over time . . . Dec. 7, 1946 . . . five years to the day after the bombing of Pearl Harbor.

If wounds were healing, every American carried the grim memory of a relative or friend who died in World War II.

And no servicemen were welcomed back to the Illinois bosom with such anticipation as basketball's original Whiz Kids—Andy Phillip, Gene Vance, Ken Menke and Jack Smiley.

These were my heroes of the time. As a sophomore at nearby Monticello, where The Game was popularized by native son Harry Combes, basketball was taking the community by storm. This was a new beginning. Huff Gym, barely 20 miles away, would be the center of the universe.

The Whiz Kids, remember, had swept the Big Ten title by three games as sophomores in 1942, and were widely proclaimed the nation's premier team when they went 17-1 in 1943.

However, at the conclusion of that wondrous season, which ended with Phillip scoring 40 points against Chicago, and just as the fifth annual NCAA tournament was beginning, duty called.

Now, more than three and a half years later, they would join forces again in an opener against an overmatched Cornell team. And the Whiz Kids weren't alone. Dike Eddleman, the state's "greatest athlete of the first half-century," was on a roster that included Walt Kirk, Fred Green and Jack Burmaster.

But a war-related illness slowed Phillip. And coach Doug Mills, in his final season, struggled to find the old chemistry. The Illini avenged an opening loss at Wisconsin by blitzing the Badgers 63-37 at home, but fell one game short of the Badgers in the title run.

Expectations unmet! A dream unrealized!

A familiar story. But if the thrill is in the chase, if the fun is in the quest, Illini fans have been well served through the years.

Basketball has remained this state's most popular sport, propelled downstate by the fervent belief that the University of Illinois is just around the corner from something great.

Promise has always been a close associate. Dating to 1935, when Combes became a sophomore starter on a Big Ten co-championship team, the Illini finished among the top three in the conference in 18 of 22 years, and reached the Final Four under Combes in 1949-51-52.

A senior-laden 1953 team, with junior Red Kerr in the middle, figured to be the best yet ... but lost a 74-70 overtime game at Indiana, and the Hoosiers went on to take the Big Ten and national titles.

Right then, as a senior at the UI, it seemed to me that Illini basketball success would be never-ending. Illinois held a clear edge over every Big Ten rival, an advantage that none would overtake for another 20 years.

But high-quality opponents, many of them featuring Illinois products, crowded the path to the top.

Combes' superb teams in 1955 and 1956 ran afoul of an Iowa Fab Five featuring Illinoisans Carl Cain, Bill Schoof, Bill Seaberg and Sharm Scheuerman.

The UI's 1963 co-champions, led by Dave Downey and Bill Small, were bumped from the tournament by NCAA champion Chicago Loyola. Combes' 1965 and 1966 clubs scored 100 or more on 25 occasions, but this was the era of Chicagoan Cazzie Russell at Michigan.

And so it has gone through the years ... quality teams ... great fan support ... unending excitement ... and the ultimate success just a finger-snap away:

• Combes' best-yet club of the 1960s, shortly after a big win at Kentucky, came apart when Rich Jones and Ron Dunlap were lost in the wake of the "slush fund" scandal in December of 1966.

• Harv Schmidt had Illini fandom in the palm of his hand with a 19-5 club in 1969, only to see his recruiting efforts backfire.

• Resurrecting a down program, Lou Henson put the Illini in the NCAA tournament eight times in the 1980s, but the 1989 run to the Final Four was followed closely by the year-early departures of Nick Anderson and Marcus Liberty, and a long NCAA investigation.

And here we are again, with new coach Bill Self inheriting a veteran squad that will be carrying high expectations into the 2001 Big Ten race.

Take it from here, Bill.

THE 1914-15 ILLINI WENT 16-0 AND WON THE NATIONAL
CHAMPIONSHIP, HOLDING THEIR OPPONENTS TO 13 POINTS
A GAME. IT WAS ONE OF TWO BIG TEN TITLES WON BY COACH
RALPH JONES.

Unbeaten Illini Head East

MARCH 6, 1915
BY THE CHAMPAIGN DAILY GAZETTE

CHICAGO—The unbeaten Illinois basketball tossers safely tucked away the conference championship Saturday night by defeating the Chicago five 19-18 in Bartlett gymnasium.

The game was the scrappiest of the season and, although the Illini left the floor at the end of the first half on the little end of an 11-9 score, they worked wonders during the second period.

The Woods brothers—Ralph and Ray—are in large part responsible for the Illinois victory. Ralph Woods succeeded in caging the winning basket scarcely a minute before the closing gun was fired.

Edward Williford was the high-point winner for Illinois. The forward's harvest was seven free throws.

The Maroons, who had lost 20-12 to Illinois earlier in the season, jumped into the lead on a basket a minute after the opening gun. Ray Woods evened the score, but the Maroons retaliated with four points. The Chicago players spurted at critical times throughout the half on free throws and baskets.

Coach Ralph Jones' men returned on the floor for the second half with genuine Illinois determination. Ralph Woods, in his eagerness, became one of the principals in what resulted in the calling of a double foul.

The outcome of the game was wholly uncertain and the two teams alternated in the lead until the very last minute of play when Ralph Woods' basketball spelled victory for the conference champions.

Illinois improved to 11-0 in conference play, three full games ahead of Chicago and Wisconsin.

LOU BOUDREAU HAD HIS NUM-
BER RETIRED—IN BASEBALL. BUT
THE BASEBALL HALL OF FAMER
ALSO STARRED IN BASKETBALL,
HELPING THE ILLINI WIN THEIR
FIFTH BIG TEN CHAMPIONSHIP IN
1936-37.

Basketbrawl

JANUARY 18, 1937
BY EDDIE JACQUIN
NEWS-GAZETTE SPORTS EDITOR

L AFAYETTE, Ind.—Captain Bob Riegel, Harry Combes, Wilbur Henry, Jim Vopicka and Hale Swanson were first-graders, Louie Boudreau was in kinder-garten and coach Doug Mills was about to receive his grade school diploma when Illinois last defeated Purdue on its home court.

But youngsters will grow up, and the full bloom of their manhood found them transformed into Fighting Illini of the first degree Monday night as Purdue was beaten 38-37 in a battle that was the survival of the fittest and included everything in the roll call of excitement and melodrama.

It was Illinois' first win at Purdue in 14 years and the Boilermakers' first loss of the season.

While the Illini, trailing 23-11 at halftime, were surging back into the game, the Jefferson High School crowd became unruly. A gym packed beyond capacity with Purdue adherents hooted, booed and jeered in a typical display of poor Purdue sportsmanship.

Coach Piggy Lambert catapulted himself onto the floor to dispute several calls. The result of it was that when the winning basket had been dumped in by Swanson, a few Purdue followers rushed the Illini as they left the floor.

Henry took several blows to the head as he seemed to be the primary target of the group. Coach Doug Mills prevented Henry from swinging back and, in the process, received a poke to the jaw. Trainer Matt Bullock, rushing into the melee, forced three or four of the foes back in none-too-gentle manner and, by this time, a pair of policemen cleared a lane for the Illini.

It was a disgraceful exhibition and adds another smudge to the already discolored picture of Purdue sportsmanship.

Swanson entered the game for the first time when Riegel fouled out with 30 seconds left and Purdue ahead 37-36. Boudreau missed two foul shots, the second of which was rebounded and put back in by Swanson. Boudreau scored 10 points and Riegel and Henry added nine points apiece.

University of Illinois Archives

FROM LEFT, ANDY PHILLIP, COACH DOUG MILLS, JACK SMILEY, KEN MENKE, VIC WUKOVITS AND GENE VANCE RUN THROUGH A DRILL. LATER, THEY BECAME KNOWN AS THE WHIZ KIDS.

The Whiz Kids Arrive

JANUARY 3, 1942
BY EDDIE JACQUIN
NEWS-GAZETTE SPORTS EDITOR

MADISON, Wis.—The defending champions of the Big Ten started out just as they did a year ago. They lost their first game. But this defeat tonight in Wisconsin's fieldhouse, 55-40, sounds a clarion note around to the far corners of the conference.

The Illinois sophomores, with yeoman help from senior Vic Wukovits and junior Art Mathisen, will have considerable say in the final reckoning in March.

Shooting with deadly accuracy to cage 24 baskets in 79 shots, handling the ball brilliantly, and sticking like veterans to their defensive chores, the youthful Orange and Blue quintet showed no sign of stage fright, buck fever or anything else that usually is expected from a bunch of boys averaging 19 years in age.

Ken Menke, Andy Phillip, Gene Vance and Jack Smiley, four of the classiest prep players in the state of Illinois two years ago, outscored everything Bud Foster's veteran quintet had to show. They traveled at a mad pace for all but the last three minutes of the game, when they stalled and picked up two baskets as they drew out the Badgers.

"They all looked good to me," Foster said of the Illini. "Speed and shooting ability are hard to cope with. They must have hit a third of their shots."

From his guard position, Phillip, a dribbling demon, scored 14 points to take the spotlight away from John Kotz, labeled by many as the best sophomore in the Big Ten last year. Kotz was guarded by Smiley, who held him to 13 points.

Menke and Mathisen each racked up 11 points for the Illini. Menke threw in one-hand shots and rebounded brilliantly, a department in which the Illini were far more effective than at any time in their conference competition.

"These four sophomores will have a merry three years if the war doesn't catch up with them," Foster said. "But Mathisen was the boy who gave us the works when we weren't expecting it."

University of Illinois Archives

WHEN POLLED, THE WHIZ KIDS PICKED THEIR
1942 WIN AGAINST GREAT LAKES AS THEIR
MOST MEMORABLE GAME, EDGING THE 1943
WIN AGAINST NORTHWESTERN.

Going Out in Style

MARCH 3, 1943
BY PAT HARMON
NEWS-GAZETTE SPORTS EDITOR

CHAMPAIGN—Chicago, which couldn't have beaten Champaign High School, came to George Huff gymnasium Monday night to furnish the valedictory chapter to the Illinois Whiz Kids for the duration.

The Whiz Kids—Mr. Phillip of the U.S. Marines, Mr. Vance of the ROTC, and Mr. Mathisen, Mr. Menke and Mr. Smiley of the U.S. Army—kept the game from being an anticlimax for 6,398 fans by setting a flock of new records in a 92-25 rout.

Never before had a Big Ten team scored 92 points in a game. Never before had a Big Ten team scored 41 baskets in a game. Never before had a team won a Big Ten game by such a wide margin.

The Illini not only did that, they set records of 755 points and 325 baskets for one season.

It all added up to another championship for the invincible Illini, their second in succession. They are the first team since Purdue in 1930 to go through the conference unbeaten (12-0) and the first team since Wisconsin in 1914 to take two straight undisputed championships.

Next to their own undefeated record the Whiz Kids took pride in having Andy Phillip break all the records he could. He made 40 points, a record for one game. He made 16 baskets, another record. He wound up with 255 points and 111 baskets, both records for a season. And he smashed Chuck Carney's own Illinois record by boosting his two-year conference total to 414 points.

In short, Phillip broke five records in one night. And that in itself is a record.

The Whiz Kids have more games to play, if they go to the NCAA tournament. And all of them but Mathisen have more years of eligibility in which to grind out new, unheard of scoring records. But to all intents, this was their last home appearance for the duration of the war, and they were out to make the most of it.

The slaughter must have made the poor Chicagoans feel like Christians thrown into the lions' den. They were helpless as the fans cried for points . . . and more points.

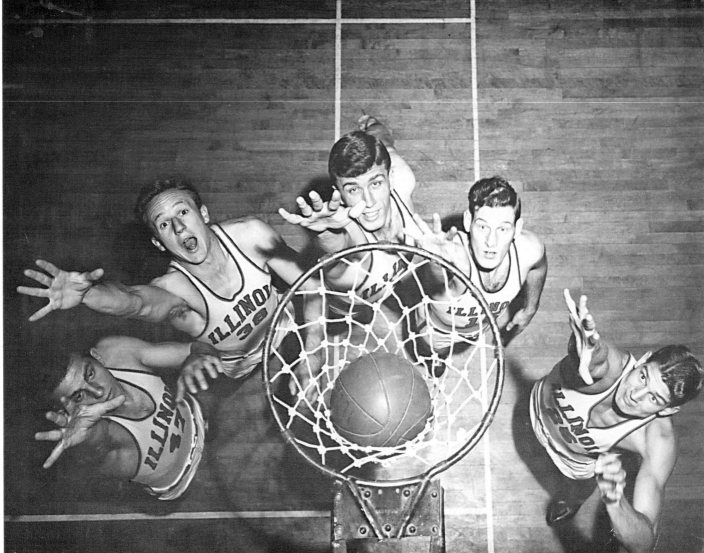

The News-Gazette Archives

FROM LEFT, ANDY PHILLIP, KEN MENKE, ART MATHISEN, JACK SMILEY AND GENE VANCE COMPRISED THE STARTING LINEUP OF THE WHIZ KIDS, ONE OF ILLINOIS' MOST FAMOUS TEAMS.

WHIZ KIDS

TEAM FOR THE AGES

BY BOB ASMUSSEN

They recount their ailments as if they were old war wounds.

Hip replacement for one. Bad heart for another.

But they endure. Just like their nickname.

They will reunite again next summer. Like always. It takes more than a bad ticker or bum knee to slow down the Whiz Kids.

Fifty-eight years ago, the Illinois Whiz Kids started a two-year domination of the Big Ten. Using quickness on offense and a sticky defense, they went 35-6.

They were at their best in conference games, winning 25 of 27 while taking consecutive league titles.

"We didn't even know what the NCAA was," Jack Smiley said. "We just wanted to win the Big Ten."

They didn't just win it. They owned it.

NEW TROOPS ARRIVE

As the 1941-42 Illini opened their season, there was no reason to expect anything special. Illinois was coming off a 13-7 season and had to replace three starters.

Four sophomores joined the varsity that season. Ken Menke, Andy Phillip, Smiley and Gene Vance formed the foundation for one of college basketball's greatest teams.

They got along like brothers. There were no egos, no ruffled feathers.

"We played the game because we loved the game," Phillip said. "We didn't have an attitude problem."

The older players didn't have any trouble sharing the spotlight. Senior Vic Wukovits and junior Art Mathisen started up front.

Maybe they got along because they had no choice. Money was tight, so they were all happy to be in college. The war in Europe and the Pacific was on their agenda.

"We came from very difficult times," Mathisen said. "Our family didn't have a car. I had to hitchhike down to Champaign."

FAST START

The 1941-42 Illini opened the Big Ten season with a 55-40 win at defending national champion Wisconsin.

The players began to believe. Consecutive wins at Michigan and Ohio State added to their confidence.

"We started beating some good teams, then it started hitting us we could keep going," Phillip said.

A seven-game Big Ten winning streak ended with a five-point loss at Indiana.

Another four wins put the Illini in position to win the Big Ten title, which they did with a 63-49 rout of Northwestern in front of 19,000 and Gov. Dwight Green at the old Chicago Stadium.

Menke finished with 19 points. Phillip and Smiley each added 13.

"They had great ballplayers," Smiley said of the Wildcats. "They could score. The defense we had was superior. We played a first-class team, a fine team, and yet we came up with that margin."

ROUGH FINISH

The 1941-42 season didn't end the way the players hoped. One game after clinching the Big Ten title, they lost by 14 at Iowa.

The Illini came back home and squeezed past Purdue 34-32. For all the players knew, the season was over. Though they had earned a spot in the NCAA tournament, there was no guarantee they would make the trip.

"It was a nonchalant thing by everybody," Phillip said. "(Coach) Doug Mills indicated we probably wouldn't go, so we all went home. He called us back and said, 'We're going.' We didn't have any practice, and we weren't really geared for it."

The NCAA tournament in '42 wasn't the extravaganza it is today, just eight teams making it.

The Illini dropped a two-point game to Kentucky in the first round at New Orleans. Penn State beat them by seven in the third-place regional game.

That was it for the Whiz Kids and the NCAA tournament. Two games. No wins. No whining.

"The Big Ten was it," Phillip said. "That was our main aim, win the Big Ten Conference. The NCAA was very small then."

THE NICKNAME

All the players tell the same story about their famous nickname. A Chicago broadcaster said during an Illinois game, "Gee whiz, look at those kids go."

The next thing they knew, the Illini became the Whiz Kids.

"It stuck with us," Phillip said. "Years later, when I went to the Hall of Fame, they all remembered the Whiz Kids."

Menke, Phillip, Smiley and Vance were all about 6-foot-3, tall for players at the time. Each had a particular strength that worked well with the rest.

"The fast break was our game," Phillip said. "We were ahead of our time."

Menke, Phillip and Mathisen were the scorers. Smiley and Vance were the top defenders.

"We all had our special nights and all came through whenever we needed to," Vance said.

The News-Gazette Archives

THE WHIZ KIDS TRY TO GET BACK TOGETHER REGULARLY TO CELEBRATE THEIR
ACCOMPLISHMENTS AT ILLINOIS. ON A 1981 REUNION IN CHAMPAIGN, THEY STRUCK
A FAMILIAR POSE.

TEAM TO BEAT

The special nights kept coming during the Whiz Kids' junior year.

For the second consecutive year, the Illini beat the defending NCAA champions, stomping Stanford 38-26. Illinois started the Big Ten season with a 13-point win at Michigan. In a 12-0 league season, the Illini won by an average of 24.2 points. Only one team, Ohio State, stayed closer than 12.

"The spread that we had in '42-43, you just don't do that unless you're all playing defense," Smiley said. "They labeled me a defensive player, but the other four guys must have played awfully good, too."

The Illini did enough scoring for both teams. They put up 86 points against Northwestern and 92 against Chicago. Unbelievable numbers at the time.

"There was no one-and-one on free throws," Vance said. "No three-point shots. To score that many points in a 40-minute ballgame, we moved a lot. You just got the ball and you'd go."

As the regular season ended, the ball got deflated. The war kept the Big Ten champions out of the NCAA tournament.

Mathisen, Menke and Smiley all got called to service. Mills wasn't going to the NCAAs without his entire team.

Wyoming won the championship that year. If the Illini had been there, the Whiz Kids said, everybody else would have been playing for second.

"I think we could have walked through it," Smiley said. "We weren't even close relative to competition from below."

JACK BURMASTER, GETTING TIPS FROM
COACH DOUG MILLS, HELPED ILLINOIS BEAT
TOP-RANKED DE PAUL FOR THE FOURTH
STRAIGHT TIME. REPLACING BOB MENKE, HE
SCORED 14 POINTS.

University of Illinois Archives

Upset Special

DECEMBER 29, 1945
BY PAT HARMON
NEWS-GAZETTE SPORTS EDITOR

CHAMPAIGN—A superbly prepared Illinois basketball team stunned De Paul 56-37 before 5,097 fans Saturday night in Huff Gym.

Fighting Illini like Wallie Mroz, George Leddy, Bob Menke, Bob Doster, Jack Burmaster and Jim Seyler accomplished the seemingly impossible. They upset the No. 1 team in the country and did so decisively.

In a game that will go down as one of the great Illini achievements of all time, the Orange and Blue exercised its annual hold over De Paul. For three straight years Illinois has beaten De Paul.

De Paul, astutely handled by coach Ray Meyer, has lost eight games in three seasons. Three of those defeats came to Illinois.

The Illinois freshmen, playing a veteran team which had four holdover regulars from the 1945 national runner-up, were brilliant. They shot expertly and ran with jetlike speed. Their shooting percentage on field goals was 41.7, holding De Paul to 24 percent shooting.

Menke, with help from teammates, defended 6-foot-9 center George Mikan. Mikan scored 20 points, slightly below his average (23) but enough to keep him No. 1 in the nation.

He shot 15 free throws, making eight. Menke fouled out after 25 minutes and was replaced by Burmaster, who tied Doster for the team lead with 14 points. Mroz added 11 points, all in a brilliant second half. Seyler had five points and Leddy scored four.

The most spectacular part of Illinois' game was indomitable spirit. The Illini eager beavers scrapped tooth and nail for every loose ball. Even little Mroz, a foot shorter than Mikan, gave it the old college try when he had a jump ball with the big boy.

He didn't get the tap, of course, but a moment later he stole a pass between two De Paul players and dribbled half the length of the floor to score.

BILL ERICKSON CHASES AFTER A LOOSE
BALL AGAINST PURDUE. HIS DRIVES TO
THE BASKET HELPED ILLINOIS SET A SCHOOL
RECORD FOR POINTS IN A GAME (98).

Making Their Points

FEBRUARY 21, 1948
BY T. O. WHITE
NEWS-GAZETTE SPORTS EDITOR

CHAMPAIGN—The Illinois basketball team, completing its play on the home-court, put on a record-smashing show Saturday which 6,905 witnesses will not soon forget.

The Illini, under the new leadership of run-shoot coach Harry Combes, defeated Purdue 98-54 and:

• Set a single-game school record for points, eclipsing the previous high of 92 set against Chicago in 1943;

• Helped by Purdue, set a Big Nine record for combined points in a game (150 was the old mark);

• Missed the single-game Big Nine record by five points (Iowa scored 103 against Chicago in 1944);

• Set a record for most points scored against a Purdue team.

When Iowa set the Big Nine record, Dick Ives set the individual league record with 43 points. The impressive Illini total was amassed with no such individual performance. The two high scorers for Illinois, Bill Erickson and Walt Kersulis, combined for 32 points and nine teammates chipped in.

Erickson gave the Purdue guards trouble with his driving tactics. He was awarded seven free throws and his fancy dan passing pleased the jubilant crowd.

The home valedictory, which marked the last appearance at Huff Gym for captain Jack Burmaster and Stan Fronczak, gave the Illini an 11-1 home record. Jim Marks, who added 14 points, also might have been making his Illini farewell. He has applied for admission to Washington University medical school and, if accepted, will start his studies there in the fall.

Van Anderson tied the school scoring record with 1:05 left. Misreading the clock, he sank a long, desperation shot for a 92-50 lead. Anderson, who finished with 13 points, followed with three more free throws to complete the scoring.

Burdette Thurlby scored nine points, Fred Green and Burmaster had eight, and Dike Eddleman scored seven for the Illini, who shot 37 percent from the field and made 18 of 23 free throws.

DIKE EDDLEMAN WAS A MULTI-SPORT STAR AT ILLINOIS, CONTRIBUTING TO THE FOOTBALL, BASKETBALL AND TRACK TEAMS. EACH YEAR, ILLINOIS PRESENTS THE DIKE EDDLEMAN AWARD TO ITS TOP ATHLETES.

DIKE EDDLEMAN

THE GREATEST ILLINI

BY JEFF D'ALESSIO

Before Mike, every little boy in Illinois grew up wanting to be like Dike.

Fat chance.

Just as there was only one Jordan, there's never been another quite like Thomas Dwight "Dike" Eddleman, either. He's the only Illini to earn 11 letters for his varsity jacket, the only one who's been to the Rose Bowl, the Final Four and the Olympics, and the only one who's made the executive director of the NCAA act like a 12-year-old kid in his presence.

Cedric Dempsey was the athletic director at Arizona when he got to meet his boyhood hero at a reception before an Illini-Arizona football game a few years ago. He was so excited, he did everything but ask Eddleman to autograph a cocktail napkin.

"Dike introduced himself, and (Dempsey) stopped and said, 'I grew up in Illinois and all my life I wanted to meet Dike Eddleman because you were the front-page story when I was growing up,'" Illinois associate vice president Robert Todd said. "We stood there for about 10 minutes while he told Dike how he always looked up to him.

"It was like that wherever you went with Dike."

Almost 50 years after his heyday, Eddleman's legend lives on. It started in Centralia, where he remains a folk hero, six decades after leading the Orphans to the 1942 state basketball championship at Huff Gym. The old-timers in town still talk about that 13-point comeback in the final five minutes to stun Paris' 39-0 powerhouse. Eddleman made a bucket at the buzzer in one of the most fantastic finishes in state tournament history.

It was the first magical moment of many in Champaign for Eddleman, who was nationally known before he even got to college. His prep exploits in track (three IHSA high jump titles), basketball (a then-state-record 2,702 points) and football (captain of the 1941 all-state team) were chronicled in newspapers and magazines beyond the Land of Lincoln.

The News-Gazette Archives

DIKE EDDLEMAN AND ILLINOIS BASKETBALL COACH
HARRY COMBES TALK STRATEGY. EDDLEMAN, KNOWN
AS THE GREATEST ALL-AROUND ATHLETE IN UI HISTORY,
WON 11 LETTERS.

On February 10, 1942, shortly after the outbreak of World War II, *Look* magazine profiled him in an issue that featured a Hitler-Mussolini cover story.

Wrote Tom Meany: "His clothes set styles. Stores advertise 'Eddleman hunting caps.' A year ago, Dike turned up his trousers four inches above the ankle. Within 24 hours, so had every other youth in Centralia."

Like Dike. If I could be like Dike ...

In his book *Grass Roots and School Yards,* author Nelson Campbell called Eddleman "the most publicized high school athlete in world history."

He's up there with the college athletes, too. Eddleman's name still comes up every June, when Illinois hands out its Male and Female Athlete of the Year awards.

Or, as they've been known since 1992, the Dike Eddleman Awards.

Go to any area bookstore, and you're liable to find a copy of his autobiography, which he co-wrote with daughter Diana "Dee" Lenzi.

The title says it all.

Dike Eddleman: Illinois' Greatest Athlete.

"He was the outstanding athlete in the history of the UI," said another one of them, Dave Downey. "And the most delightful thing about him is that he never changed from the nice, simple Centralia boy he was."

It wasn't easy juggling three sports and school at the UI, but somehow Eddleman pulled it off. Things got especially hectic around the holiday season his sophomore year, when football coach Ray Eliot wanted him for the January 1 Rose Bowl in Pasadena and basketball coach Doug Mills wanted him for a tournament in Berkeley, Calif., on December 20-21.

Rather than fight over him, they agreed to share him.

Wrote the *Urbana Courier:* "Between these sports, he should play 18 holes of golf daily, beat Bobby Riggs at tennis, swim the Catalina channel, give a high jumping exhibition off the Golden Gate. We have no doubts he could do it, but we fear as soon as this happened, Hollywood would grab him for Tarzan roles."

Basketball was Eddleman's favorite sport, but he was superb at all of them at the UI, where his career was interrupted by three years of military service.

In football, he once boomed an 88-yard punt against Iowa, still holds the school record with a 43-yard average and played for the 1946 Big Ten and Rose Bowl champs.

In track, he high jumped to a silver medal at the 1948 Olympics, won an NCAA championship in his specialty the same year and helped Illinois take the team title in 1946.

In basketball, he was named Big Ten MVP in 1949, led Illinois to its first 20-win season since 1908 the same year and joined Wally Osterkorn, Bill Erickson, Burdette Thurlby, Jim Marks, Fred Green and Don Sunderlage on Harry Combes' Final Four team.

The next year, he went on to the NBA, where he played four seasons with the Tri-City Blackhawks and Fort Wayne Pistons.

"We were the pioneers of the NBA," said Eddleman, who retired to a career in business when the Pistons tried to trade him to Baltimore.

His dream job came along in 1969, when his alma mater hired him as associate director of the UI Grants-In-Aid program. During a 25-year career with the UI Foundation, Eddleman raised more than $45 million in scholarship money.

"Without a doubt, my No. 1 job has been collecting funds for the university and athletic scholarships," he said. "I never had asked for money, and it was hard at first, but I had a great reason to ask."

Eddleman retired in 1992, but still works part-time raising funds for the Fighting Illini Scholarship Fund.

"There's never been anyone who's had greater affection for the UI," Downey said.

University of Illinois Archives

ILLINOIS' WALLY OSTERKORN (13) AND DIKE
EDDLEMAN (40) LED ILLINOIS TO A THRILLING WIN
OVER MINNESOTA AT HUFF HALL, STOPPING A 14-GAME
WINNING STREAK BY THE GOPHERS.

Close Counts

JANUARY 29, 1949
BY JACK PROWELL
NEWS-GAZETTE SPORTS WRITER

CHAMPAIGN—The real Fighting Illini, the comeback kids of 1949, socked Minnesota 45-44 on Saturday in a basketball masterpiece before 6,905 hoop-happy spectators.

They say champions win the close ones. If that's true, let them sing praise to the team that may be the next champion from the Big Nine conference . . . the team that has won all the close ones: Illinois.

A difference of four points (they look as big as a thousand) today separates Illinois from the leadership of the toughest conference in the country and the cellar. The Illini are 4-0 after handing second-place Minnesota its first loss in 14 games this season.

Indiana (44-42 in double-overtime), Ohio State (64-63) and Minnesota have been victims of late Illini rushes. Illinois leads in wins because it leads in courage.

Illinois, amazingly enough, won from the free throw line. The same team that had missed 23 against Indiana made 15 of 17 against Minnesota.

Jim Marks' two free throws put Illinois ahead for good, 43-42. Marks scored the last four points in what was Illinois' first win against the Gophers since 1945.

Harry Combes' pressing defense was the difference as the Illini rallied from a 23-9 deficit. Bill Erickson's second-half pressure on Whitey Skoog took Minnesota's best right out of the ballgame.

"Erickson won that game in the second half the way he guarded Skoog. He was the best player on the floor," Illinois athletic director Doug Mills said. "It honestly looked to me like Skoog knew Erickson was a better man than he was and was afraid to shoot because he knew Erickson would make him look bad.

"You take Skoog, I'll take Erickson and I'll have the better ballplayer."

Skoog scored six baskets, five of them in the first half. Only one of his baskets came while Erickson was guarding him.

DON SUNDERLAGE
LED ALL SCORERS AT THE
1951 NCAA TOURNAMENT,
AVERAGING 20.8 POINTS A
GAME. HE'S ONE OF THE
FEW ILLINI TO APPEAR IN
TWO FINAL FOURS.

University of Illinois Archives

No Garden Party

MARCH 24, 1951
BY JACK PROWELL
NEWS-GAZETTE SPORTS EDITOR

NEW YORK—Jim Linville scored in the last 12 seconds Saturday night to hand Illinois a 76-74 defeat in the semifinals of the Final Four.

Illinois, which had led most of the way, tied the score twice in the last minute in a dramatic finish at Madison Square Garden before Linville sank a 5-foot one-handed push.

Ted Beach's free throw brought Illinois within 72-70 with 1:15 remaining. Then the fun began.

Irv Bemoras tied the score with a push shot from outside the free throw circle before Linville's hook put Kentucky ahead 74-72. With a half minute left, Don Sunderlage drove in, jumped at the free throw circle and tied the score again at 74.

By this time it was a wild scramble. Linville raced the floor, faked his guard out of position, took a pass and sank a short shot. Only 12 seconds remained.

Illinois took time out to lay its plan. Sunderlage took the shot, and the semi-hook rolled off the rim. As the gun sounded, Rod Fletcher and Linville were on the floor rolling after the loose ball.

Thus ended Illinois' dreams of a national championship. The Illini will play Oklahoma A&M in the consolation game.

The outcome was a shame because Illinois played superior basketball. It lost because Bill Spivey, Kentucky's 7-foot center, was allowed to stay in the game until the final five minutes despite obvious roughing tactics that forced Illinois' two centers to be charged with a total of nine personal fouls.

Spivey scored 28 points to lead Kentucky.

Fletcher played his greatest game for Illinois. He scored 21 points and was tremendous on the boards. Sunderlage scored 20.

Illinois' chances were dimmed in the second half when Bob Peterson, its 6-8 center, was forced to leave the game for seven minutes with four personal fouls. He then fouled out a minute after returning to action.

University of Illinois Archives

JIM BREDAR (19) STOLE THE SHOW FOR ILLINOIS
IN ITS TWO NCAA TOURNAMENT GAMES IN CHICAGO,
SINKING CLUTCH SHOT AFTER CLUTCH SHOT.

Final Four-Bound

MARCH 22, 1952
BY BILL MARSTELLER
NEWS-GAZETTE STAFF WRITER

CHICAGO—A good little man can still play big league basketball.

Jim Bredar, a 5-foot-10 guard from Salem, pulled Illinois to a 74-68 victory over Duquesne in the regional championship game of the NCAA tournament on Saturday in Chicago Stadium.

By its victory before a rather disappointing crowd of 13,641, Illinois qualifies for the Final Four in Seattle where it meets St. John's, an upset winner over Kentucky.

Bredar, Mr. Clutch for Illinois in both games here, was a brilliant shot and a superb morale builder in the second half. Held to one basket in the first half, Bredar scored seven baskets in the second half, most of them coming just when Duquesne closed to within one or two points.

Duquesne was led by its tall boys, Dick Ricketts and Jim Tucker, who combined to score 51 points.

The Illinois dressing room was bedlam after the game, but coach Harry Combes sat in a corner quietly reading the telegrams he had put down before the start.

"I'm glad that one's over," Combes said. "How about that Tucker? There's a truly fine ballplayer."

Commenting on Bredar, Combes said, "He was worth a million dollars tonight."

Rod Fletcher, having one of his really good nights both ways, helped Illinois to a 46-38 lead. But Ricketts and Tucker got hot, getting Duquesne within 59-58 and 65-64.

Then, however, the Illini caught fire again as Bredar potted a couple. Illinois led 70-65 with 6:45 left when Fletcher fouled out.

Ball holding tactics caused Duquesne to start picking up costly fouls and Illinois finished the game declining free throws.

The Illinois team credited the announcement of the St. John's victory over Kentucky as an assist.

"That was a kick," Bob Peterson said. "That helped."

JOHN KERR

BIG RED

BY JEFF D'ALESSIO

In 1952, John Kerr was named to the NCAA's first all-tournament team at Edmundson Pavilion in Seattle.

In 1979, he found out about it at a cocktail party in Atlanta.

"It's funny," Big Red said. "I was in Atlanta when Al McGuire's Marquette team won it and they had the NCAA book sitting on a cocktail table. It went back through all the Final Fours. I was flipping through it and I saw I made the all-tournament team. I didn't even know it. There was no big honor back then."

Kerr and Jim Bredar, teammates in 1952, remain the only Illini ever to receive the NCAA's high honor. For Kerr to do it was something else, considering he didn't even start on the '52 Final Four team. Harry Combes trotted out junior Bob Peterson at center instead.

But Kerr, the leading scorer of that team and every other one he played on at Illinois, didn't stay seated for long.

"I might have been one of the first sixth men in college basketball," Kerr said.

Even though the '52 Illini fell short of the final, losing 61-59 to St. John's the game before, they're still near the top of any list of great teams in school history. Like Combes' '49 and '51 teams, they finished third in the country and won an outright Big Ten title, the last UI team to do so.

That was also the year the nation started to take notice of the 6-foot-9 Kerr, a rising sopho-more who starred at Chicago's Tilden Tech and was *thisclose* to becoming a Bradley Brave. Two of his old Tilden teammates had signed with Bradley the year before and everyone assumed Kerr would follow them.

"As a matter of fact, in my high school graduation pamphlet, it had a bunch of guys with their scholarships at the bottom and it had 'John Kerr, Bradley,'" Kerr said.

Future teammate Irv Bemoras, then a star at Chicago's Marshall High, helped rewrite it. He'd already committed to Illinois and tried like heck to get Kerr to do the same.

"Irv called me and said, 'Why don't you take a train ride down and see what it's like?'" Kerr said. "That was fine with me. I didn't want to get on any planes or anything. So I took a train ride down there and God, I fell in love with the campus. I met Harry Combes and (assistant) Howie Braun and just decided that's where I was going."

It turned out to be Bemoras' greatest assist ever.

Kerr went on to become a Big Ten MVP, Illinois' all-time leading scorer and a second-team All-American.

One night on the road in 1954, he scored 38 at Ohio State, missing out on Andy Phillip's school record by a basket. Not too shabby for a guy playing on one leg.

"The funny thing was, I sprained my ankle at the start of the second half," Kerr said. "They just taped right over the shoe and I continued playing. It might have been a little higher that night."

Aside from his scoring (25.3 a game as a senior) and rebounding (they didn't keep that stat in those days, but he had a bunch), what made Kerr so special was his speed and stamina. He could run with the guards and go entire games without taking a breather, thanks to his background as a prep soccer player.

"I was tireless," he said.

He proved it at the next level, too, setting the NBA's ironman record while playing in 844

The News-Gazette Archives

JOHN KERR'S 25.3 SCORING AVERAGE IN 1953-54 RANKS SECOND ALL-TIME AMONG ILLINOIS SENIORS. DON FREEMAN AVERAGED 27.8 IN 1965-66.

straight games with Syracuse, Philadelphia and Baltimore. One of a select number of players with 10,000 points and 10,000 rebounds on their NBA resumes, Kerr later became the first coach of the Chicago Bulls, winning Coach of the Year honors in 1967.

He's spent the last 26 years calling Bull games on TV. It was a dream job during the Jordan years, but hasn't been a lot of fun lately.

"We paid a penalty the last couple of years for all the good times we had in the '90s," Kerr said.

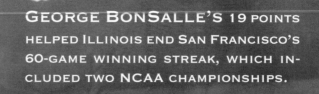

GEORGE BONSALLE'S 19 POINTS HELPED ILLINOIS END SAN FRANCISCO'S 60-GAME WINNING STREAK, WHICH INCLUDED TWO NCAA CHAMPIONSHIPS.

University of Illinois Archives

The San Francisco Treat

DECEMBER 17, 1956
BY T.O. WHITE
NEWS-GAZETTE SPORTS WRITER

CHAMPAIGN—Faced with a once-in-a-lifetime opportunity Monday, the Illinois basketball team responded with its finest performance of the season to overwhelm the San Francisco Dons 62-33 and end the longest winning streak in college basketball history.

A superb Illinois defense, coupled with an offense coordinated to escape the clutches of a team stressing protection of its goal, literally blew the Dons out of the gym and handed them their first loss since December 11, 1954, when they fell to UCLA 47-40. In between, San Francisco won 60 consecutive games and two NCAA championships, and was rated No. 1 in every poll.

It is true the team is shorn of Bill Russell, its great offensive and defensive center, and K.C. Jones, its great guard who starred with the Olympic champions, and Gene Brown, the other regular guard who is out with injury. But that was only part of the reason for the Illinois victory.

From the time George BonSalle dropped in an easy basket on a tricky pass from captain Harv Schmidt 20 seconds into the game until Larry Breyfogle ended the scoring with a late jump shot, Illinois was in complete control before 6,912 fans.

So much so that San Francisco's point total was the lowest for an Illini foe since 1949.

Don Ohl completely neutralized forward Carl Boldt, a regular last year who struggled to get five shots and was scoreless. BonSalle and Schmidt played the pivot so well that Mike Farmer, another returning regular, and two other Dons made only seven baskets in 30 attempts.

BonSalle led the Illini with 19 points and 11 rebounds. Schmidt, held to one basket, made up for his lack of scoring with 16 rebounds.

Billy Altenberger contributed eight points and picked off seven rebounds. Johnny Paul played almost half the game and, while he made only one basket, he held up his end on defense.

BOB STARNES' 50-FOOT HEAVE AT NORTHWESTERN RANKS AS ONE OF THE ALL-TIME GREATEST SHOTS IN ILLINOIS HISTORY. IT PROPELLED THE ILLINI TO THEIR LAST OUTRIGHT BIG TEN TITLE.

A Heave to Believe

JANUARY 14, 1963
BY ED O'NEIL
NEWS-GAZETTE SPORTS EDITOR

EVANSTON—Quick-draw Starnes slumps no more.

Shooting from the hip in the basketball equivalent of *High Noon,* Illinois captain Bob Starnes blasted down the bad guys of Northwestern on Monday in a fiction-style ending, 78-76. Except, if you read it in a book, you'd chortle at the writer's lack of imagination.

Shaking off the shackles of a streak as chilly as the outdoors, Starnes lifted the beleaguered Illini in another hour of need and steered them past the last ambush before semester exams with a 26-point outburst.

He topped the performance off with a shot that will be burned into the Illini memory book before this ink is dry!

It was a 21-karat, gold-plated jim-dandy that he uncorked as the zeroes ran together on the McGaw Hall clock to keep third-ranked Illinois' conference record perfect at 4-0.

With two seconds to go, the Illini had a tie score and the ball under their own basket. The whole length of the purple-bordered floor was between them and victory.

Starnes took two dribbles and took a shot that went missile-straight through the goal a good 50 feet away.

The Illini, who didn't lead for a second in the game before Starnes' payoff pump, would have been happy to settle for overtime just seconds before.

For Starnes, caught in the clammy claws of a slump that saw him score only 30 points in four games, it was a moment to equal his 28-point performance against New York University in Madison Square Garden.

His push-hook-throw touched only net, and official Remy Meyer left no doubt of his view of the play. He signaled it good immediately, not checking anyone else's opinion.

A Northwestern turnover with six seconds left created the opening for Starnes. Bill Small called a timeout and, after four seconds elapsed, Illinois got it, just before Dave Downey's shot from midcourt nearly went in.

Downey scored 20 points and Small scored 14.

Photo courtesy of Dave Downey

DAVE DOWNEY GOES UP FOR TWO AGAINST INDIANA'S JIMMY RAYL. DOWNEY SCORED 53 POINTS AGAINST THE HOOSIERS, SETTING A BIG TEN SINGLE-GAME RECORD. A WEEK LATER, RAYL SCORED 56.

Downey's Day

FEBRUARY 16, 1963
BY ED O'NEIL
NEWS-GAZETTE SPORTS EDITOR

BLOOMINGTON, Ind.—Dave Downey exploded for 53 points in the greatest one-man show ever put on by an Illinois player but his but companions couldn't keep pace as the Illini blew a 103-100 decision to Indiana on Saturday.

Despite Downey's fantastic performance of 22 goals in 34 shots, the Illini wasted a lead that was as large as 12 points in the first half and eight with 10:45 to play.

No other Illini could manage as many as a dozen points in support of Downey's brilliant game which broke:

• The Big Ten record for points in a regulation-time game (held by Purdue's Terry Dischinger with 52);

• The conference mark for field goals (22 to 20 for Michigan's John Tidwell, Indiana's Jimmy Rayl and Dischinger);

• The Illinois school point mark (40 by Andy Phillip in 1943); and

• The school goal record (16 by Phillip in 1943).

Downey's 27-point first half propelled Illinois. He rammed in 26 more in the second half, but the rest of the Illini attack turned to milk toast.

Downey made 9 of 9 free throws and led the Illini with 13 rebounds.

Tom Bolyard and Rayl combined for 63 points for Indiana, making 23 of 27 charity shots.

Four Illini fouled out. The killing blow came when Skip Thoren was sent to the bench with five fouls with 10 1/2 minutes from the finish line.

Winning the field goal duel by 10, the Illini got only six shots from the foul line in the second half, even though Indiana guarded them man-to-man throughout the period.

Bill Burwell, who scored 51 points in two games against Indiana last year, was virtually helpless. He put in 4 of 19 shots and blew nearly a dozen soft touches.

The loss pushed the Illini back into a tie for the league lead with Ohio State, pressing hard for its fourth straight championship.

THREE-TIME ILLINOIS
MVP DAVE DOWNEY
WAS AS GOOD A
REBOUNDER AS HE WAS
A SCORER, SETTING A
SCHOOL RECORD WITH
21 IN 1961 AGAINST
CREIGHTON.

DAVE DOWNEY

ONE OF A KIND

BY JEFF D'ALESSIO

Tough to say which Dave Downey was better at: basketball or business.

Before going on to become a world-famous leader in the insurance industry, Downey was a pretty fair forward. He came from á little coal town, but could match moves with any of his big-city teammates and opponents.

"One of the ultimate compliments I was ever paid was from Don Freeman, who was a shy guy and didn't really have a lot to say," Downey said. "He came over to me one day and said, 'Dave, you ain't all white.'

"And I said, 'Thank you.'"

Downey's proud to say he picked up some of what Freeman called his "bag of tricks" from Govoner Vaughn and Mannie Jackson, the first two African-Americans to wear orange and blue. They were seniors when he was a freshman at Illinois in 1959-60, and they taught him as much about basketball as Harry Combes did.

Three years later, Downey had a similar impact on Freeman, another African-American star-in-waiting who broke his mentor's scoring record.

"I played every night in practice against Govoner, and Don played every night in practice against me," Downey said. "That legacy passed over about a 12-year period of time, and that was an important change in Illinois basketball. That was the beginning of the modern era."

Better leapers and sharper shooters have come along since, but Downey will forever be remembered by Illini fans. For leading Combes' 1963 team to a share of the Big Ten title. For joining Deon Thomas and Kiwane Garris as the only three-time team MVPs in school history. For scoring 1,360 points in three seasons, 13th-best all-time.

Photo courtesy of Dave Downey

DAVE DOWNEY (40) STILL HOLDS THE UI'S SINGLE-GAME RECORD FOR
FIELD GOALS WITH 22—FIVE MORE THAN ANDY KAUFMANN AND EDDIE
JOHNSON.

And, of course, for the single-most impressive performance in 95 years of Illinois basketball.

It happened at Indiana's Assembly Hall, of all places, where another great moment in Illini history would go down 26 years later. If you thought Nick Anderson's shot in '89 was something special, you should have seen what Downey did to the Hoosiers on February 16, 1963.

You'd never be able to tell it from the footage, but he wasn't feeling his best that day. The plane ride over on the DC-3 had been a little on the choppy side, leaving Downey so ill he missed the pregame shootaround.

Later, after watching Downey score a Big Ten-record 53 points against their Hoosiers, thousands of Indiana fans were the ones with the sick stomachs.

"It's been almost 40 years," said Dick VanArsdale, a star on that Hoosier team. "The only thing I remember about that game is that I wasn't the one guarding him."

Indiana beat Illinois 103-100 that day, but

all anyone was talking about afterward was Downey, who went 22 for 34 from the field, 9 for 9 from the line and berserk on the boards, grabbing 15 of them.

No Illini's come close to his 53-point day since. Andy Kaufmann is next on the UI list with 46 against Wisconsin-Milwaukee in 1990.

And Kaufmann had the three-point shot to help him. That wasn't yet a part of college basketball in Downey's days.

"Some years ago, I was given a videotape that had been made from the old 16-milimeter film of the game," Downey said. "You can't tell for sure where the three-point line would have been, but I had six or seven shots that probably would have been three-pointers in today's game."

No Big Ten player had ever scored more points than Downey in a non-overtime game. Until seven days later, that is, when Indiana's Jimmy Rayl lit up Michigan State for 56 on 48 shots.

But record or no record, the performance was a pivotal one in Downey's career, making it easier for him to walk away from basketball six weeks later with a smile.

"It allowed me to get on with my life," he said. "Most athletes, regardless of when you stop playing—whether it's in junior high or high school or college or professionally—you always think, 'If I could have played one more, I could have played a little better.' I looked at that one and said, 'I couldn't do any better than that.' "

Downey played eight more games after the Indiana one, then hung up his high-tops for good, a move he's never regretted. Never ever.

He could have been a pro but passed, going the law school route instead.

"I had very good counsel at the time," he said. "Marty Blake, the NBA's superscout, was

the general manager of the St. Louis Hawks back then. The NBA was not a big deal. In those days, they had regional and territorial draft choices. There were only eight teams in the league. He talked with me quite a bit and said if I was going to play, they would draft me first, which would have made me the third or fourth person chosen.

"We talked about it and he asked me my career alternatives. I told him I was planning to get married and that I had been accepted into a couple of very good graduate programs—the MBAs at both Harvard and Yale—and I thought about that, but wasn't going to do it. He said to me, 'If you were my son, I would say go ahead and get whatever education you can. Get on with your life because there are people who can't do anything else and will kill for the positions in the league.'

"He said, 'You're the wrong size, but you're a good shooter and you're smart and you'll probably be able to hang around the league for a while. But you're going to have to do something else anyway, so if you were my son, I'd say go ahead and do it.' "

And so he did, turning down a $12,500-a-year offer with the San Francisco Warriors, who picked him in the fourth round of the 1963 draft. He had a chance to get back into basketball a few years later when Red Auerbach's Celtics were looking for a forward, but Downey, married and in law school with a son on the way, passed again.

The UI's 1988 Varsity I Award winner is as big a star in the community as he was in college. He serves on numerous boards, works as an adjunct professor of finance at the UI and is one of Champaign's biggest success stories.

"It's hard to imagine I could have had a better life than I've had," Downey said.

University of Illinois Archives

THE ASSEMBLY HALL, WHICH OPENED IN 1963, IS THE
BIG TEN'S THIRD-OLDEST BASKETBALL BUILDING, BE-
HIND MINNESOTA'S WILLIAMS ARENA (1928) AND
NORTHWESTERN'S WELSH-RYAN ARENA (1951).

A Grand Opening

MARCH 4, 1963
BY ED O'NEIL
NEWS-GAZETTE SPORTS EDITOR

CHAMPAIGN—Illinois launched the mammoth, magnificent Assembly Hall to the tune of a nail-biting 79-73 victory over Northwestern on Monday.

A crowd of 16,137 came to cheer the home forces, marvel at the spectacular building and listen to the serenading of a 110-piece band.

But shabby play on both sides, provoked by two added musical starters performing a duet on whistles, made it less than a rousing sendoff of the Hall. The basketball was ordinary and the officiating was the same.

While the two teams were hitting 43 goals, the referees mistook the largest crowd ever to see a game in the state outside of Chicago as a welcoming committee for striped clothing. They called 57 personal fouls and turned the evening into a march in waltz tempo from one end of the floor to the other. Those fouls resulted in 88 free throw attempts—more than two a minute.

Dave Downey, struggling for his points, collected 19 to lead the Illini along with Bill Small. Downey put in two free throws with 5:13 left in the first half to account for his fifth and sixth points and break John Kerr's all-time career scoring record.

He added 13 in the second half to make the new figure 1,313. He has one more game to embellish his mark.

Free throws were all the Illini got in the final three minutes, but they made 10 of 11 to keep the Wildcats at bay. Northwestern got only one goal in the final 3:30, that by Rantoul's Bill Gibbs, who strung together 11 charity tosses for a 17-point night.

The roundhouse turned out to be safe after all.

As athletic director Doug Mills consoled coach Harry Combes, he said: "At least you have a streak going here, even if it's only one game."

Construction on the Assembly Hall began in 1959. The building was completed in 1963 at a cost of $8.35 million.

SKIP THOREN WAS ONE OF ILLINOIS' STARS AT THE 1963 L.A. CLASSIC, WHERE HE SET A SCHOOL RECORD WITH 24 RE- BOUNDS AND MADE THE ALL- TOURNAMENT TEAM.

Chairman of the Boards

DECEMBER 28, 1963
BY ED O'NEIL
NEWS-GAZETTE SPORTS EDITOR

L OS ANGELES—UCLA's Bruins, who want to be No. 1 in the country, might not even be No. 1 in the Big Ten. And surprise, Illinois might be a powerful contender for the title it shared last year.

Harry Combes' courage kids, down by as much as 14 points in the second half, battled back and had a chance to tie the Bruins with six seconds left in the game before falling 83-79 in the L.A. Classic finals.

Skip Thoren, who set a school record with 24 rebounds, was named to the all-tournament team. Thoren's rebounding effort bettered that of Dave Downey and Bill Burwell. Downey had 21 rebounds against Creighton in 1961 and Burwell reached that mark against Wisconsin two months later.

Thoren wasn't even around at the end. The Illini got so close even though Thoren and another team leader, Tal Brody, fouled out.

Bob Brown, a seldom-used sophomore deadeye from West Frankfort, hit two goals in the last 90 seconds to bring the Illini close. After Brown, Jim Vopicka, Mel Blackwell, Larry Hinton and Bogie Redmon scrambled back into contention, they couldn't get the one break they needed.

The margin was 79-78 with 20 seconds left when UCLA ace Walt Hazzard made two free throws. Blackwell then was called for an offensive foul on a play that could have gone either way. But Brown refused to quit and ticked the ball away from Hazzard, and Vopicka was fouled picking it up.

With six seconds to go, Vopicka made his first to make it 81-79. Then he intentionally missed, hoping Don Freeman could take the rebound. Instead, UCLA got it and a long-court heave gave the Bruins their final margin.

It was almost a miracle moment for an Illini team which must have been a 20-point underdog. And it gave the Illini great hope for a conference race, since favored Michigan was beaten 98-80 and crushed completely here Friday night.

The News-Gazette Archives

JIM DAWSON, LEFT, WITH COACH HARRY COMBES AND TEAMMATE DON FREEMAN, ENJOYED A SPARKLING DEBUT IN ILLINOIS' IMPRESSIVE ROMP OVER DEFENDING CHAMPION UCLA.

Something's Bruin

DECEMBER 4, 1964
BY ED O'NEIL
NEWS-GAZETTE SPORTS EDITOR

CHAMPAIGN—Battle-tested Illinois, collecting some lovely dividends from the hard-earned lessons of last year, demolished defending national champion UCLA on Friday in what coach Harry Combes called the "greatest opening game in my memory and one of the best Illinois games, period."

The Illini tore up the pressing defense which was UCLA's trademark last year in winning 30 straight games, and 58-percent shooting took care of the rest in the 110-83 triumph.

There were no real individual heroes, just a tremendously balanced and poised bunch of grizzled performers all clicking at once.

In the opening game for both teams, the Illini used no magic . . . just torrid shooting and tremendous execution of their game plan. Bill McKeown, a senior guard from Clinton who had his season ended by a broken arm a few days after winning regular status last February, keyed the early going as the Illini raced to a 52-38 lead.

Soon it got to the point that no matter which player Combes inserted, the efficiency remained the same. Skip Thoren scored 20 points, McKeown 19 and Bogie Redmon and Don Freeman 17 apiece.

Jim Dawson scored nine points in his first game. St. Joseph-Ogden's Deon Flessner also played well in his varsity debut.

"I was asking a little of Dawson and Flessner to throw them in against the national champions in their first game, but they held up just fine," Combes said. "That Flessner walked in there like he belonged and played tough, sound defense."

The Illini set an Assembly Hall record for points and missed the school record by a basket. Six Illini reached double figures.

"I'm pleased with the depth and with the intelligent game our kids played," Combes said. "When they started to slip a little bit (after the 25-point lead with 15 minutes left) they got back to doing the things that got them the lead the first time."

HARRY COMBES IS ONE OF THREE ILLINOIS COACHES TO RANK AMONG THE TOP TEN IN THE BIG TEN WINNING PERCENTAGE. COMBES WON 61.9 PERCENT OF HIS GAMES. RALPH JONES WON 67.4, DOUG MILLS 65.2.

The News-Gazette Archives

HARRY COMBES

AHEAD OF HIS TIME

BY LOREN TATE

Few athletic success stories among the "smalltown-boy-makes-good" vein will top Harry Combes'.

It all started for Illinois' second-winningest coach at Monticello High School in the 1930s. The Sages won 52 of 56 games during his last two seasons and he was an athlete of sufficient talent to take the giant step which few smalltown players make: he attended the state university and led the Illini in scoring, making the All-Big Ten teams in 1936 and '37.

He was just as good as a coach.

Combes' career kicked off in 1939 at Champaign High School, where the gym was later named in his honor. In the period leading out of World War II, he incorporated a magnetic personal intensity with a revolutionary running, pressing style to lay waste the opposition in an incredible 13-year stretch.

"It really took a lot of teams by surprise," former Maroon Ted Beach said. "I remember one of our games at Huff Gym against Urbana, the first time they saw the press in '45. They only got one point in the first half."

During his last four seasons at Champaign High, Combes' Maroons competed in three state championship games—winning it all in 1946 with a 54-48 triumph over Centralia. That team remains the last from the Champaign-Urbana area to be crowned state champs.

After a 254-46 nine-year run at Champaign, Combes moved to Illinois, where he had similar success, never finishing worse than third in the Big Ten his first nine years. His Illini won the Big Ten in 1949, '51 and '52, and came in third in the NCAA tournament all three years, twice losing to Kentucky in the semis.

Former Illini Fred Green remembers the transition year in 1947-48, when Combes inherited a veteran group of players from Doug Mills at Illinois. Green was a center on that club, which was captained by Jack Burmaster and also featured Wally Osterkorn, Dike Eddleman, Burdette Thurlby, Jim Marks, Skip Kersulis, Bill Erickson, Van Anderson and Dick Foley.

"Some of those younger players weren't much younger than Harry, but he really had no difficulty," Green said. "Harry was a straight shooter and devoted student of the game. He had been a great innovator in high school and he brought the free-wheeling game to Illinois. He wanted us to get a shot as quickly as possible, and he wanted it to be a good shot.

"Harry used a lot of players those first two years and while I was more substitute than starter, I felt very much a part of it. He brought in the press and used it less often than in high school but with a lot of success. We departed from Doug Mills' four-man figure-eight off the pivot and went to a quicker offense.

"As the years wore on, Harry showed that he could recognize talented players and he knew how to let them do their thing."

Combes' records from 1948-56 were 15-5, 21-4, 14-8, 22-5, 22-4, 18-4, 17-5, 17-5 and 18-4.

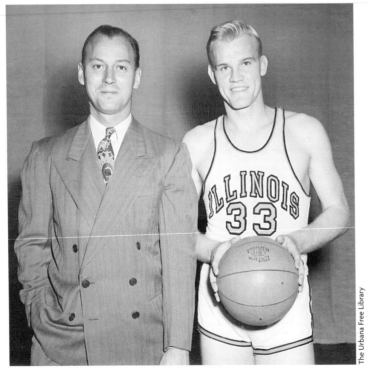

HARRY COMBES, SHOWN HERE WITH BILL ERICKSON, ALSO COACHED CHAMPAIGN HIGH TO ITS ONLY STATE TITLE IN 1945-46. HE WON 254 GAMES IN NINE SEASONS.

The Urbana Free Library

Jim Wright, who played alongside Red Kerr from 1952-54 and later assisted Combes, says there was only one Harry.

"Aside from my father, there is no man whose word I would believe more wholeheartedly than Harry," Wright said. "His word was his bond. Athletes who played for him sensed this integrity.

"As a coach, he had the ability to bring out the best in his players. He would explain what he wanted—and he chewed us all out at one time or another—but he had a way of keeping everyone's confidence up.

"Harry believed that you could overcoach players, and he tried to avoid that. He let the athletes do what they could do best. He was called a run-and-gun coach, but he also coached the defensive end. He liked to change the tempo of the game by hitting a team with a zone press or a man-to-man press."

Combes, who died on November 13, 1977, at the age of 62, was a a great coach fully deserving of his national Hall of Fame award. But he was not destined to go out on top, as a series of misfortunes dotted his last 11 seasons at Illinois.

First came the George BonSalle incident, the star center going ineligible just as he reached a level of performance which figured to lead Illinois into strong contention for the 1957 championship.

Then came a string of recruiting failures with blue-chip athletes who were emerging in Chicago: Marshall superstar George Wilson chose Cincinnati in 1960 and Carver's Cazzie Russell selected Michigan.

Combes suffered his first, and only, losing season in 1961, but did it with a group of promising sophomores who rose around the leadership of Dave Downey and Bill Small to share the Big Ten title in 1963. Flush with that success, Illinois recruiting picked up and,

HARRY COMBES, RIGHT, TAKING A RIDE WITH DON SUNDERLAGE, WON THE BIG TEN'S MEDAL OF HONOR IN 1937.

after the high-scoring Skip Thoren-Tal Brody club went 18-6 in 1965, the stage was set for a title run in 1966-67.

Combes' last team featured Rich Jones, Steve Kuberski, Ron Dunlap, Jim Dawson, Dave Scholz, Preston Pearson and Deon Flessner, and they served their coach with a revenge victory against Kentucky in December of that season.

But slush fund revelations struck the campus a few days later, assistant athletic director Mel Brewer turning over records indicating a systematic program of illegal payments to football and basketball players.

"I've always maintained—and I really feel I know for sure—that Harry was by far the most innocent person in the slush fund episode, and it ended up hurting him more than it hurt anybody else," Downey said.

Jones, Kuberski and Dunlap were declared ineligible and Combes' final team sagged to 12-12, handing its coach a rousing 80-70 win over Big Ten champion Indiana in his last home game at the Assembly Hall.

Combes finished 316-50 in 20 seasons at the UI—second all-time to only Lou Henson (423-224).

"Harry Combes was a relatively small man in a game of giants," said former UI football coach Ray Eliot, who delivered his eulogy. "He had to have a great courage, fortitude, state of mind and, of course, the will to win."

The News-Gazette Archives

ADOLPH RUPP WAS BESIDE HIMSELF AF-
TER ILLINOIS UPSET HIS KENTUCKY WILDCATS
IN THE CHAMPIONSHIP GAME OF THE KEN-
TUCKY INVITATIONAL TOURNAMENT.

Bluegrass Special

DECEMBER 19, 1964
BY ED O'NEIL
NEWS-GAZETTE SPORTS EDITOR

LEXINGTON, Ky.—A satisfied Harry Combes pulled heavily on his soft drink, smiled wearily and exhaled. He had just had the last big blank in a brilliant coaching career filled in by his Fighting Illini.

A victory over Kentucky was one laurel that had eluded him. Considering it was only the 143rd time in more than 34 years that Adolph Rupp's teams have lost, Combes must have had a lot of company, but that was little consolation.

Rupp, as runner-up at the Kentucky Invitational Tournament, performed the traditional ceremony of presenting the huge trophy to Combes, and it was a moment a man remembers for a long time. A deathly silence hung over the UK Memorial Coliseum, where seconds before the Illini had held off the Wildcats 91-86 before 11,800 fans.

"Both teams looked pretty tired there at the end," Combes said.

Skip Thoren scored 27 points and Tal Brody had 25 as the Illini got the best of Kentucky stars Lou Dampier and Pat Riley. Two Dampier baskets brought the Wildcats within 83-82 before Brody sank two clutch free throws. It was the last threat to the Illini.

Illinois made 10 consecutive free throws to become the first Big Ten team to win the tournament.

"Illinois has a very experienced team and they do not panic," Rupp said. "If anything we were outguessed on our offensive maneuvers. We had to protect our boys against Thoren. He was just too big for us."

Larry Hinton also made two big free throws for Illinois down the stretch.

"We haven't been a good free throw team all season but we sure were when it counted tonight," Combes said. "It was the way they were falling in for us in the first half. When the ball does that you hurt any kind of defense.

"In the last minute or two, it took more than a little guts to step up there in all that noise and put them in."

PRESTON PEARSON, WHO LATER WENT ON TO STAR WITH THE DALLAS COWBOYS, HELD HIS OWN ON THE BASKETBALL COURT, TOO. ONE OF PEARSON'S MOST MEMORABLE WINS WAS THE 1966 THRILLER AT MICHIGAN.

Conquering Cazzie

FEBRUARY 1, 1966
BY ED O'NEIL
NEWS-GAZETTE SPORTS EDITOR

ANN ARBOR, Mich.—Illinois ended six years of major sports frustration against Michigan on Tuesday night with a wild 99-93 upset victory that turned the Big Ten championship tussle into a horse race and gave Harry Combes a most memorable 300th victory as a college coach.

Don Freeman and Rich Jones turned in superhuman efforts and the rest of the Illini battled tooth and nail with them to subdue the two-time defending conference kings.

They did it the hard way in one of the most inspired games any Illinois athletic team has ever played, shaking off foul problems that had Preston Pearson and Deon Flessner in four-personal trouble before the half and Freeman with three.

All of these things they overcame with a crowd of 7,350 Michigan partisans screaming in their ears in antiquated Yost Fieldhouse.

Down three points at halftime, the Illini detonated their greatest shooting display in a single half, firing a phenomenal 69.7 percent in the last 20 minutes and ramming in 57 points.

When it came time for someone to crack, it was supposedly pressure-proof Michigan that did. The Wolverines wavered long enough to allow the Illini to surge into the lead, and Illinois wouldn't crumble.

Freeman scored 33 points and Jones had 31. For Freeman, cementing a strong bid for All-American honors, it was a satisfying night as he matched Cazzie Russell point-for-point, shot-for-shot, heroics-for-heroics.

Russell, who scored 33 points, made three major mistakes in the showdown stages of the game, forcing shots and throwing the ball away. He scored four points in the final eight minutes.

Jones survived a nasty fall after colliding with a Michigan player. Claiming he never lost consciousness when his head hit the floor late in the first half, Jones nonetheless needed five minutes before he could stand up.

DON FREEMAN

THE MADISON MARVEL

BY JEFF D'ALESSIO

The governor couldn't make it to Don Freeman's final home game as an Illini.

So Otto Kerner sent along his director of public safety instead.

Hey, someone from the state had to be at the Assembly Hall to present the proclamation declaring March 5, 1966, Don Freeman Day all across Illinois.

"I'll always remember that day," said Freeman, who now works for the Federal Reserve Bank in Houston. "There was a heck of a snow the night before and it seemed like my whole hometown came up, anyway. We were playing Iowa. I think I had a good game, but I can't recall."

Hard to forget. The guy they used to call "the Madison Marvel" scored 32 points that day and Illinois blasted the Hawkeyes 106-90, capping off one of the most spectacular senior seasons in school history.

Thirty-four years later, Freeman's name is still all over the UI record book. The 6-foot-3 forward averaged 27.8 points a night as a senior, easily a school record. His 668-point total is also the best in school history—by eight (Andy Kaufmann had 660 in 1991).

"It's still the record?" said Freeman, who figured Eddie Johnson had him beat. "I can't believe that."

Freeman, who left Illinois that year as the school's career scoring leader, ranks ninth on the all-time list, despite playing just three years.

In his day freshmen were ineligible, which didn't bother Freeman a bit. He had a lot to learn about big-time basketball and picked up plenty of pointers just from watching the 1962-63 varsity team from the stands.

The star of that Big Ten championship bunch was the one and only Dave Downey, the guy Freeman would later replace as Illinois' all-time leading scorer. As a kid growing up in Madison,

Freeman used to love to watch Govoner Vaughn and Mannie Jackson. Then he got a load of Downey, and it was like, Govoner who?

"I guess he was my favorite, a guy I kind of styled myself after. I just really enjoyed watching him," Freeman said. "Dave had a bag of tricks. He could hang and do some of the things that the pros do now back then. He could move, change his shot and still make it. He was my favorite."

Freeman was no slouch himself, leading some of Illinois' highest-scoring teams in points. Harry Combes' Illini were the Loyola Marymount of their day, ringing up 92.2 points a night during Freeman's junior year and 87.4 his senior year.

Those totals still rank Nos. 1 and 3 all-time at the UI.

"Harry Combes was a run 'n shoot type coach," Freeman said. "I think our team would fit in with the style of play today."

To this day, Freeman remains one of only two Illini in history to average 20-plus

The News-Gazette Archives

ONLY NICK WEATHERSPOON ENJOYED A BIGGER GAME AGAINST MICHIGAN THAN DON FREEMAN. HIS 33 POINTS HELPED ILLINOIS DELIVER A WIN IN ANN ARBOR IN 1966.

points and 10-plus rebounds a game for his careers, cementing his status as one of the all-time greats. Nick Weatherspoon also pulled it off.

Freeman was even more productive as a pro, scoring 12,233 points for the NBA's Los Angeles Lakers and ABA teams in Miami, San Antonio, Utah, Dallas and Indiana, where he

won a championship. Among ex-Illini, only Eddie Johnson, Derek Harper and Red Kerr put up more points at the next level.

"I can't say that he's better than Red Kerr or Don Sunderlage or Dave Downey," Combes once said of Freeman. "But he's as good as any of them. The game changes so much, you can't compare eras."

University of Illinois Archives

RICH JONES, MIDDLE, WAS ONE OF 12 ILLINOIS
ATHLETES SUSPENDED BY THE SCHOOL AS A RESULT
OF ITS SLUSH FUND INVESTIGATION.

Troubling Times

DECEMBER 23, 1966
BY LOREN TATE
NEWS-GAZETTE SPORTS EDITOR

The penalty which Illinois has feared the most—more than being eliminated from postseason competition, more than loss of TV revenue, more than the suspension of its coaches—has happened with the announcement that the university has withdrawn from competition 12 current basketball and football players.

In another of its continuing acts of good faith during the self-started investigation of financial payments to athletes, Illinois suspended five basketball players, including varsity members Rich Jones, Ron Dunlap and Steve Kuberski, before a game against California in Chicago.

Coach Harry Combes said he planned to appeal the university's suspensions. Earlier in the day, he offered his resignation to Illinois president David D. Henry.

Just as he had refused football coach Pete Elliott's resignation almost two weeks ago, Henry said he wished Combes to continue.

"If our administration had to take action, I wish they had taken it against me and not the players," Combes said. "This is a terrible price for the boys to pay. It could change the course of their lives. They were all completely stunned when I told them they could not play for Illinois."

Of the 12 players currently under suspension, seven were football players. The 17 others who received illegal aid since 1962 have completed their eligibility. University records show $21,000 was dispersed to athletes for a variety of reasons in 1962.

Prof. Leslie Bryan, UI interim athletic director, reiterated that the length of the suspensions is indefinite and was made with the agreement of the Big Ten commissioner's office. At the same time, Big Ten commissioner Bill Reed emphasized the conference is continuing its investigation and will hand down a decision in early March.

The NCAA action is expected to come later and, by past standards, could very well be more severe and long-lasting than the Big Ten ruling.

HARV SCHMIDT'S SECOND ILLINOIS TEAM ROARED TO A 10-0 START, INCLUDING AN IMPRESSIVE WIN AT HOUSTON, WHICH HAD WON 60 CONSECUTIVE GAMES AT HOME.

Streak Busters

DECEMBER 21, 1968
BY LOREN TATE
NEWS-GAZETTE SPORTS EDITOR

HOUSTON—Illinois survived two knockout punches and a savage Houston rally attempt to break the Cougars' 60-game home winning streak, 97-84, in Delmar Gym on Saturday.

The convincing triumph extended Illinois' pre-Christmas win streak to seven and stamped the team's bid to be ranked among the nation's top 10 this week. Houston had been 31-2 the previous season, including a win against Illinois.

Randy Crews and Jodie Harrison were flattened on the court and temporarily dazed by the muscular hosts in the rugged second half. But the Illini, ahead 50-39 at the break, hung on grimly with clutch free throw shooting midway in the second half and breakaway goals near the end.

Theodis Lee drew an intentional foul for slugging Harrison with the score 68-61 with 9:38 remaining. At this point, Illinois missed three golden opportunities when Rick Howat fell on the humidity-slick floor, Fred Miller's driving layup spun out and Howat missed from 15 feet.

But Illinois refused to buckle, contesting the Cougars for every basket and chopping into the 1-3-1 zone defense.

Greg Jackson scored 21 points for Illinois, including a conventional three-point play after a pass from Miller that made it 85-73 with two minutes remaining. It marked only the second time in second-year coach Harv Schmidt's era that anyone other than Dave Scholz topped the 20-point mark.

Scholz matched Jackson's 21 points though playing almost all the second half with four fouls. Fouls also hampered Mike Price, who started opposite the remarkable Ollie Taylor before fouling out with 16:40 to go. Taylor scored a game-high 28 points.

Illinois shot 38 percent from the field but made 31 of 35 free throws. Houston was outrebounded 54-41 and committed 21 turnovers.

The win improved Illinois to 7-0 ahead of next week's Hurricane Classic in Miami.

NICK WEATHERSPOON

SILVER SPOON

BY JEFF D'ALESSIO

The '70s didn't bring any Big Ten titles, NCAA tournament trips or 20-win teams. But Illinois fans still had a reason to show up at the Assembly Hall back in those days.

His name was Nick Weatherspoon—or just plain "Spoon," as most folks called him—and he was a joy to watch.

"He had a lot of crowd appeal," said Harv Schmidt, who recruited him out of Canton, Ohio, and coached him in Champaign. "The name was catchy and he played so hard. He had a flamboyant air about him. Just extremely confident."

Despite playing for teams that won just 39 games in three years, Weatherspoon went down as one of the most popular—and productive—Illini of all-time.

"Spooooon," they used to chant when he did something spectacular. Which was about, oh, every other possession or so.

"He had as good a turnaround jump shot as you're going to see from 12 to 15 feet around the basket," Schmidt said. "He could shoot the turnaround both ways and he had great jumping ability. He could really get up over people."

Once he did, it was usually over. No Illini in history could put up points like the Spoon, whose 20.9 career average is better than Deon Thomas', better than Don Freeman's, better than Dave Scholz's, better than any of them.

"He was a really quiet guy," former UI teammate Rick Schmidt said. "He didn't really say anything to anybody on the team. Except 'Gimme the ball.'"

His teammates were always happy to oblige, helping Weatherspoon finish fourth in the Big Ten scoring race as a junior and second as a senior.

The News-Gazette Archives

NICK WEATHERSPOON WAS THE SECOND ILLINI
EVER TO BE PICKED IN THE FIRST ROUND OF THE
NBA DRAFT, THE WASHINGTON BULLETS SE-
LECTING HIM WITH THE 13TH PICK IN 1973.

He was No. 1 all-time at Illinois for eight years, too, breaking Scholz's school scoring record during a win over Northwestern on March 5, 1973. When he scored the record basket, the game was stopped and the crowd went crazy.

Weatherspoon went, "Huh?"

"When that big roar went up, it kind of scared me," said Weatherspoon, who wasn't much into records. "I was running back on defense and didn't know what was happening. No one said anything about stopping the game."

He was glad they did. It gave him an opportunity to pick out his mom in the crowd, run over to her and give her the game ball.

Ruby Weatherspoon had plenty to be proud of. Not only could her son score, but he was a Rodman-like rebounder, becoming the only Illini in history to average double figures in that department three straight years. He grabbed 23 one night as a sophomore against Michigan, missing Skip Thoren's school record by one. He had 22 two years later against DePauw. He averaged 11.4 for his career—almost five more a game than Efrem Winters, Illinois' all-time leading rebounder.

And he did it at 6-foot-6 and 195 pounds.

"Nick was unusually strong," said former Illini Dave Downey, who enjoyed broadcasting his games. "He was thin and wiry, but very, very strong."

His bony build led many to believe he wouldn't be able to survive with the big bangers in the pros. But Weatherspoon, a first-round pick of the Bullets in 1973, did OK for himself after leaving Illinois, scoring 4,056 points and hauling in 2,232 rebounds in eight seasons with Washington, Seattle, Chicago and San Diego.

He made it to the NBA Finals as a Bullet in '75, playing sixth man on a team that featured Hall of Famers Elvin Hayes and Wes Unseld.

"I don't remember who it was, but somebody said to me when they saw him the first time, 'He'll never play with those rubber bands for legs,' " former Celtics coach Tommy Heinsohn said. "They were wrong."

LOU HENSON STARTED HIS ILLINOIS
COACHING CAREER ON A ROLL, WINNING
HIS FIRST FIVE GAMES AGAINST NE-
BRASKA, KENT STATE, MISSOURI-ROLLA,
NEW MEXICO AND NORTH DAKOTA STATE.

Lou's Debut

NOVEMBER 28, 1975
BY LOREN TATE
NEWS-GAZETTE SPORTS EDITOR

LINCOLN, Neb.—Lou Henson, a deceivingly forceful fundamentalist who has made a specialty of turning sick programs into healthy ones, enjoyed an auspicious coaching debut with Illinois on Friday.

The underdog visitors pulled a stirring 60-58 upset of Nebraska as 6-foot-9 sophomore Rich Adams capped a 25-point performance with a tiebreaking jumper from the corner with eight seconds to go.

The outcome stunned a crowd of 6,235 in Lincoln's ancient coliseum. Working carefully for close-in shots, the Illini hit the hoop at a 53-percent clip and forced the Cornhuskers away from the hoop with a 2-3 zone which Henson installed only a week ago. The defense contributed to Nebraska's 42 percent shooting and overloaded wherever 20-point scorer Jerry Fort roamed, limiting the All-Big Eight guard to 10 points.

"When you hold a veteran team like Nebraska to 58 points, you must be doing something right defensively," Henson said. "We'd only been working on that 2-3 zone for about a week. We just figured that, being on the road and all, it might be the best idea."

Adams racked 19 of his points after intermission, converting 10 of 13 field goals and five of seven free throws. The southpaw, who moved into the starting lineup after an impressive showing with the second team in a practice game at Chicago Heights Bloom, scored 16 of his team's final 20 points.

"Rich did a fine job," Henson said. "He took good shots, worked on defense and got on the boards.

"Actually, we didn't execute the offense as well as I would have liked. But it's tough playing your opener on the road and nursing such a small lead all the time."

Otho Tucker added 18 points as Henson became the sixth consecutive Illinois coach to win his debut. It didn't come easy: Inclement weather forced the Illini to land in Omaha, Neb., and take four cars to Lincoln.

FIGHTING ILLINI

ILLINOIS	MSU
55	55

PERIOD 2

0:04

PLAYER
FOUL NO

DEREK HOLCOMB (44) LOOKS
UP AS EDDIE JOHNSON'S
CORNER JUMPER GOES THROUGH
THE NET TO BEAT NO. 1-RANKED
MICHIGAN STATE.

Shot in the Arm

JANUARY 11, 1979
BY LOREN TATE
NEWS-GAZETTE SPORTS EDITOR

CHAMPAIGN—A young, starless University of Illinois basketball is No. 1 in the nation today.

Oh, sure, the polls don't come out until next week. And the Illini could be beaten by then—rugged Ohio State is the foe Saturday.

But just ask any of their orange-waving fans. The Illini are No. 1 because on Thursday night, playing before the largest crowd in UI history, they outfought, outrebounded and outscored No. 1 Michigan State 57-55.

It took a last-ditch corner jumper by sophomore Eddie Johnson to do it, but this was a game that the Illini controlled after a nervous beginning. A jumper by that same Johnson—Eddie, not Magic—sent the Illini ahead 47-46 with 9:25 left and they never trailed thereafter.

With the game tied at 55, the Illini won a jump ball and held for the final shot. As the clock dipped under 10 seconds, Steve Lanter found room down the middle and passed off to an open Eddie Johnson in the corner.

"I knew it was going in when it left my hand," the grinning Westinghouse forward said. "That's my favorite. I didn't know how much time was left but I knew somebody had to shoot, and it happened to be me."

It was the shot heard 'round the nation. The victory extended the nation's longest winning streak—15—and set the stage for another showdown of 3-0 conference teams when Ohio State visits.

"We can't afford to celebrate," UI coach Lou Henson said.

On Johnson's game-winner, the coach added: "I was happy to see him put it up from there. That's his favorite. When we huddled, we didn't specify anyone to take the shot. We just wanted to work the ball under 10 seconds and let the first open man shoot."

The spectacular ending made the crowd of 16,209, including Gov. James R. Thompson, forget the shaky beginning in which the Illini fell behind 24-13 to the defending Big Ten champions.

EDDIE JOHNSON

MR. AUTOMATIC

BY JEFF D'ALESSIO

Eddie Johnson came to Champaign in the fall of 1977 thinking he was pretty hot stuff.

Nothing a few weeks under Lou Henson couldn't fix.

"I've always said that the one thing Lou Henson did for me was when I came from Westinghouse as the No. 1 player in the state, he put me right on the bench," Johnson said. "It tore down my ego, but I stuck with it and worked on my game. I truly believe if I would have fought that, I probably wouldn't have been in the league as long as I was or I wouldn't have been as productive."

No ex-Illini was as productive in the pros as the hard-working Johnson, who put up 19,202 points in 17 seasons with Kansas City, Sacramento, Phoenix, Seattle, Charlotte, Indiana, Denver and Houston. Illinois' third all-time leading scorer ranks 30th all-time in the NBA, ahead of names like Magic, Maravich and McHale.

Not too shabby for a second-round draft pick who came off the bench most of his career.

"One thing has never changed with Eddie, and that's his character," said Henson, his old coach. "Eddie wasn't even a first-round draft choice. But he is a strong-willed person who worked to overcome his shortcomings and he has always been tough in the clutch."

Never tougher than on January 11, 1979, when Johnson hit what was known for years to Illinois fans simply as The Shot. It came with four seconds left, beat the No. 1-ranked, national championship-bound Michigan State Spartans and sent 16,209 fans home happy and hoarse.

Eddie, not Earvin, was the only magic Johnson at the Assembly Hall that day.

"It was probably the biggest game that happened in Champaign," said Johnson, a sophomore that season. "There was so much at stake. We could be No. 1 in the country."

But after starting their season by winning their first 16, Henson's Illini finished it by dropping 11 of their final 15, tumbling from the polls and missing out on the postseason.

The News-Gazette Archives

AFTER RETIRING FROM BASKETBALL, EDDIE JOHNSON (33) WENT INTO BROADCASTING. THE FORMER NBA IRONMAN HAS WORKED BOTH COLLEGE AND NBA GAMES.

"I was just so embarrassed by how it turned out for us," Johnson said.

Even though they fell apart like a soggy souffle, the Illini's 19 wins that year were their most since the 1969 season. After a decade of dormancy, they were on the verge of something special.

In Johnson's junior year, the Illini advanced to the NIT Final Four and won 22 games, their most since '52. The next season, they earned their first NCAA tournament berth in 18 years.

Illinois basketball was back, and no one had more to do with it than Johnson, who left campus as the school's all-time leading scorer (1,692) and rebounder (831). He held the scoring record for 12 years after taking it from teammate Mark Smith, who didn't mind giving it up.

"I think I was more proud of the mark," Johnson said. "Mark wasn't a stat-conscious player. I always have been an offensive player. I think it meant a lot more to me than it would to him.

"It wasn't a competition thing. We were roommates. It was just something that happened. We didn't dwell on it."

The NBA's Sixth Man of the Year in 1989, Johnson retired from basketball 10 years later. He's stayed involved in the sport by broadcasting college games and wouldn't mind getting into coaching someday.

"I'm going to be more successful in life after basketball than I was during basketball," Johnson said. "Oh yeah. There's no doubt about it. That's what you go to school for."

JAMES GRIFFIN AND THE ILLINI ADVANCED TO THE NIT SEMIFINALS IN NEW YORK CITY WITH WINS AGAINST LOYOLA, ILLINOIS STATE AND MURRAY STATE. THEY WOUND UP IN THIRD PLACE.

John Dixon, The News

Ready or Not, Here Illinois Comes

MARCH 13, 1980
BY LOREN TATE
NEWS-GAZETTE SPORTS EDITOR

CHAMPAIGN—Ready or not, New York City, here we come!

"Ballad of the Illini" lyricist Fuzzy DeLisle won't challenge Cole Porter. Our Chief Illiniwek isn't a real Indian. And our basketball team won't strike up comparisons with the Philadelphia 76ers.

In fact, these Illini cagers couldn't make free throws Thursday (5 for 16).

But they're the darlings of this long-depressed athletic community. They hung on to eliminate Murray State 65-63, thereby qualifying for a berth in Monday's semifinal round of the NIT in Madison Square Garden.

The Illini, celebrating their first 20-win season in 17 years, will join Virginia, Minnesota and UNLV in New York.

Yes, they did it the hard way . . . with customary scoring leader Eddie Johnson starting 0 for 6 and finishing 4 for 15 . . . and by missing seven free throws with a potential of 13 points in the last 5 1/2 minutes.

But who expected it to be easy? These Illini, making their first postseason appearance since 1963, lost 12 games this season. But they have magic going outside the Big Ten, having won 13 consecutive games in holiday and postseason tournament play, and building a highly respectable 25-2 non-Big Ten record the last two seasons.

On Thursday, Perry Range and Johnson each missed free throws that would have sealed the win. Murray State's Jerry Smith had one last shot to tie the game, but his 35-footer hit the back of the rim as time expired.

"We won the game under adverse conditions, we won it the hard way," Illinois coach Lou Henson said. "If we could have just made some free throws, I thought we could have stayed up by 10 to 12 points."

Range and Reno Gray scored 16 points apiece. Smith had 10 points and Johnson nine for Illinois, which got six points, six rebounds and a strong defensive effort from Derek Holcomb. Henson also was pleased with the turnout (15,070).

"The crowd really helped us," he said.

University of Illinois Archives

MARK SMITH HAD A TOUGH DAY FROM THE FIELD, BUT MADE UP FOR IT AT THE LINE AGAINST WYOMING IN THE NCAA TOURNAMENT, SINKING 8 OF 8 FREE THROWS.

How Sweet It Is

MARCH 14, 1981
BY LOREN TATE
NEWS-GAZETTE SPORTS EDITOR

L OS ANGELES—Lou Henson's Fighting Illini, true to the comeback pattern that carried them into the NCAA basketball playoffs, survived a coast-to-coast Saturday of stunners to reach the Sweet 16.

"I've never seen a day quite like this one," said Henson, his voice barely audible due to a throat virus. "When you see some of the teams that lost, we have to feel very fortunate to be advancing."

On an afternoon that will be remembered as the day once-beaten powerhouses De Paul and Oregon State met disastrous upsets, the Illini squeezed past Wyoming 67-65 to reach the Sweet 16 in its first NCAA tournament game since 1963.

Senior forward Mark Smith changed from goat to hero by sinking the tiebreaking free throws with three seconds remaining.

Thus the Illini extended their glowing record of courageous finishes, dating back to a stirring comeback at Marquette in December and carrying through memorable Big Ten triumphs at Michigan State (71-70) and Ohio State (63-57) and at home against Michigan (67-64).

Perry Range's 15-foot jumper tied the game at 65. Smith then was fouled by Ken Ollie after grabbing Bill Garnett's missed shot. A Wyoming timeout failed to shake Smith, who needed to make amends for seven turnovers and 3-of-8 shooting.

"I knew I'd make them because I had rhythm at the line all day," said Smith, who finished 8 of 8.

Eddie Johnson scored 19 points for the Illini, who got 14 points from Smith and 12 from Craig Tucker. Illinois advances to play Jack Hartman's Kansas State Wildcats in Salt Lake City.

"We beat one of the top teams in the country," Henson said. "We led most of the way, and when we fell behind I told the players, 'We're not going to be front-runners. Let's fight back and win it.'

"It was the kind of rough, tough game we expected and we feel fortunate to have won."

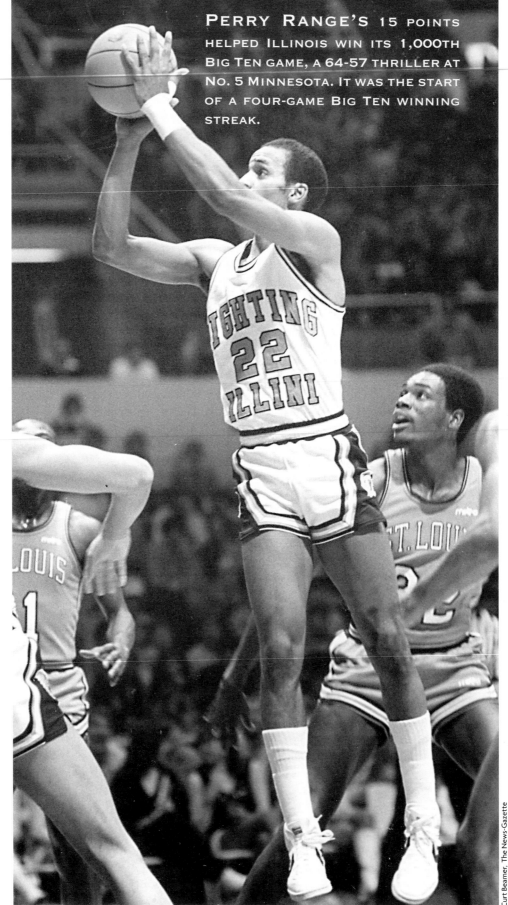

PERRY RANGE'S 15 POINTS HELPED ILLINOIS WIN ITS 1,000TH BIG TEN GAME, A 64-57 THRILLER AT No. 5 MINNESOTA. IT WAS THE START OF A FOUR-GAME BIG TEN WINNING STREAK.

Curt Beamer, The News-Gazette

Hard to Believe

JANUARY 23, 1982
BY LOREN TATE
NEWS-GAZETTE SPORTS EDITOR

MINNEAPOLIS—Lou Henson's Fighting Illini won the hard way Saturday. All the pregame factors pointed toward Minnesota's nationally fifth-ranked Gophers. The Illini had lost a heartbreaker Thursday to Indiana, were worn down by a frustrating 13-hour trip Friday and were somewhat surprised by Henson's benching of ace guard Derek Harper.

But Harper played a blistering 38 minutes and the Illini outhustled the tall Gophers 64-57 as 6-foot-10 James Griffin outscored 7-3 Randy Breuer 19 to 15.

"We feel fortunate to beat this team," said Henson after Illinois' 1,000th Big Ten game.

Illinois wins in Williams Arena have been infrequent, the Illini sending the home folks away disappointed three times in 17 contests dating back to 1964.

"Minnesota was very sharp in the first half, and it would have been easy for our guys to get discouraged after that heartbreaking loss to Indiana," Henson said. "Breuer was causing us serious problems with his size, and they hurt us with those long bombs from outside.

"But we kept battling and that's a great credit to the players. Harper came in and did a fine job. He's not in any trouble. We just wanted to make a point."

A glistening .568 shooting percentage was accomplished despite another dismal 1-for-10 outing by Craig Tucker. But it was Tucker who kept Minnesota at bay with five crucial free throws in the final 2 1/2 minutes.

"We boxed out and came up with the loose balls," Tucker said. "On the free throws, I didn't think about anything except putting the ball in."

Perry Range helped the Illini, now 3-3 in Big Ten play, with 15 points on 5-of-7 shooting.

"This was a do-or-die game for us," Range said. "If we had lost, we'd have been down at the bottom of the pack."

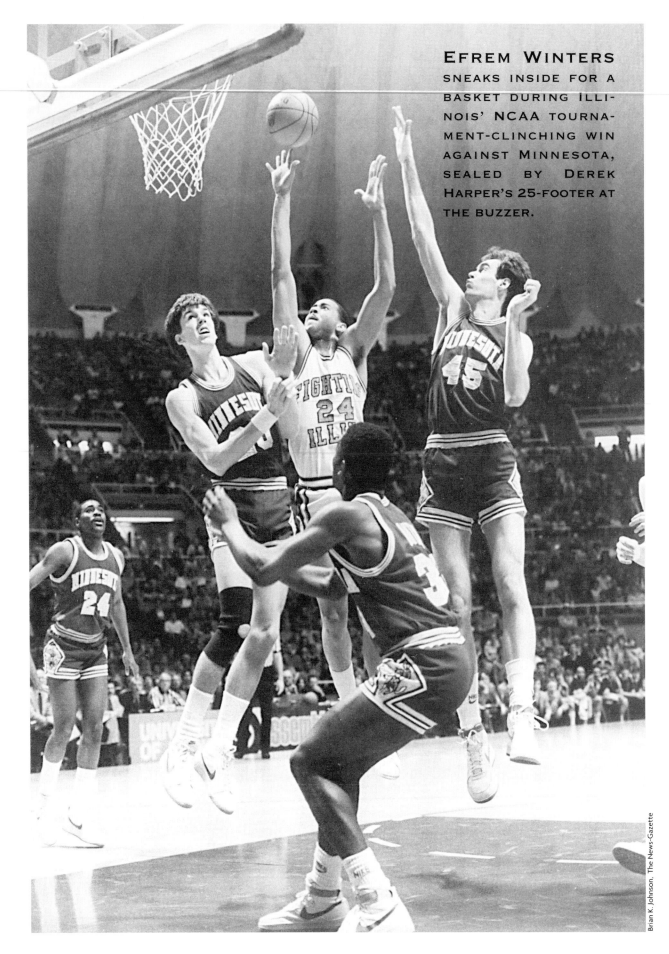

EFREM WINTERS SNEAKS INSIDE FOR A BASKET DURING ILLI-NOIS' NCAA TOURNA-MENT-CLINCHING WIN AGAINST MINNESOTA, SEALED BY DEREK HARPER'S 25-FOOTER AT THE BUZZER.

Buzzer Beater

MARCH 13, 1983
BY LOREN TATE
NEWS-GAZETTE SPORTS EDITOR

CHAMPAIGN—Boise, Idaho?
To Lou Henson, that's Paris in the springtime, New Orleans during Mardi Gras. Henson's Illini fought Minnesota's northern giants through two nerve-tingling overtimes Sunday, won 70-67 on Derek Harper's 25-foot jumper at the end of the 50th minute and joyously accepted an NCAA bid to meet Utah on Thursday in distant Boise.

"This is a tremendous accomplishment for a young team to fight back from those early 26-point losses at Minnesota and Oklahoma and tie for second in the Big Ten and reach the NCAA playoffs," Henson said. "That was one of the goals we had set. Boise sounds awfully good to me."

Sunday's hard-fought victory capped a stirring 21-10 season that began in November in Anchorage, Alaska. It was a season that saw the Illini grow steadily, with no serious slumps, from a 58-47 opening loss to Vanderbilt. Despite heartbreaking losses to Purdue and Iowa, the Illini prevailed in their only three overtime games and garnered a dozen triumphs by eight points or less.

"No, we didn't talk about the NCAA tournament back then in December, not with the guys so young," Harper said. "I knew we had a lot of ability."

With the game tied at 67 with 11 seconds left in the second overtime, Minnesota's Jim Peterson missed from 18 feet out and the Illini gained possession. After timeouts at :08 and :04, Harper took the inbounds pass from midcourt, forced his defender back with his dribble and popped from 25 feet. It hit nothing but net.

The crowd of 15,386—including many fans who stayed over from the Class A boys' tournament—went wild.

"We shot too early," Minnesota coach Jim Dutcher said. "We were looking for something under five seconds. Those were the instructions but, unfortunately, they weren't carried out."

WHEN HE LEFT SCHOOL, DEREK HARPER WAS THE UI'S ALL-TIME LEADER IN ASSISTS AND STEALS. HARPER FINISHED 23 POINTS SHY OF 1,000 IN THREE COLLEGE SEASONS.

Curt Beamer, The News-Gazette

DEREK HARPER

"SWEET D"

BY JEFF D'ALESSIO

Tacked on to the end of the biggest local sports story of 1980 was this little nugget of news:

"Interest in Derek Harper was such that *The News-Gazette* sports phones were shut off for the first time ever, just so the two-man morning sports staff could complete work on the afternoon editions. The switchboard operator estimated that she fielded more than 50 calls on Harper before noon."

They called from all over all day and all night on April 16, 1980, all wanting to know if what they'd heard was true—that Harper, the No. 1 high school guard in the nation, was headed to Illinois.

The surprise signing of Illinois' first McDonald's All-American created as big a stir as the announcements of Nick Anderson or Frank Williams or any of the other high school hot shots who followed Harper in later years.

More than 150 schools recruited the pride of West Palm Beach, Fla., including Michigan, where Harper would have wound up had coach Johnny Orr not split for Iowa State; Florida State, whose coach at the time, Joe Williams, raved, "Derek is the best high school guard I've ever seen"; and Florida, which spent more than $100,000 chasing Harper.

Illinois shelled out a few bucks on him, too, Lou Henson sending assistant Tony Yates to the Sunshine State once a week since his campus visit in early December.

"On 21 straight Tuesdays—I'm serious—I flew out of Champaign, Ill., on the same flight and made the same connection out of Chicago to West Palm Beach, Fla.," Yates said. "I got to know all the flight attendants, and they all knew me."

Turns out Harper was worth the effort.

They called him "Sweet D"—and not just because of his first name, either. Few Illini in history could play defense like Harper.

Butkus, Hardy, Rice . . .

"Derek probably had the quickest hands I've ever seen on a college athlete," Yates said.

DEREK HARPER
IS ONE OF EIGHT ILLI-
NOIS ALUMS TO PLAY
IN AN NBA FINALS.
HIS NEW YORK KNICKS
LOST TO THE HOUSTON
ROCKETS IN 1994.

The Illini knew they were in good hands with Harper, who as a freshman in 1981 led them to their first NCAA tournament berth in 18 years. He did it again as a junior, kicking off a string of eight straight NCAA berths for Henson's gang.

Many longtime followers, including former Illini Fred Green, think Harper is the school's best point guard ever. Most think he's the school's best pro ever. Some even consider him the school's best player ever.

"The thing with Harper was his magnificent physique, and he was so quick," Green said. "He could play with anybody, anytime, anywhere."

"When other players would make mistakes, he would make up for them because of his quickness," said Bennie Louis, captain of Illinois' 1967 team.

And when point guards on other teams made mistakes, he'd make them pay, picking off a pass or just plain snatching the ball away from them. He led the Big Ten in steals twice and had the two highest single-season totals in school history (72, 67) until a couple guys named Bruce and Battle came along.

Harper left Illinois as the all-time leader in steals and assists, and might still be up there had he decided to hang around for his senior season. But after averaging 15 points, leading Illinois to another 20-win season and hitting 57 percent of his shots in Big Ten games as a junior, Harper felt it was time to make a move.

His 10 brothers and sisters and single mother in West Palm Beach needed money, and Harper had an opportunity to make a whole bunch of it.

"Financially, my mother needs help," he said at the time. "Nine of my sisters and brothers are at home. It's not easy for her to support them alone. There are phone bills and the rent to pay and food to buy."

And what if his family lived on easy street instead of Seventh Street in the projects?

"I would have stayed in school," Harper said.

No one was happier to hear his decision than ol' mom, who started planning her new lifestyle immediately.

"First of all, I need somewhere to live," Wilma said at the time. "Then I'll pay off the cars, buy some new clothes and get a lifetime membership to the spa."

Without their best player, Henson's 1983-84 Illini still managed OK the next season, winning 26 games and a piece of their first Big Ten championship in 21 years.

"Who needs Harper?" fans wondered.

"Quinn Richardson filled in and had a great senior season," Henson said. "But people who say we were just as good without Harper are overlooking what an outstanding player he would have been that year. I would have liked to see what we could have done if we had had him."

The NBA move turned out to be a smart one for Harper, who the Dallas Mavericks took with the 11th pick in the 1983 draft. Harper was as big as Staubach in Big D, going on to become the franchise's all-time leader in assists (5,111), steals (1,551) and three-pointers (705) in his 11 1/2 seasons there.

He also put in time with the Lakers, Knicks and Magic, and ranks seventh all-time in NBA history in steals (1,957).

"There's not a bad thing I can say about the guy," Mavericks general manager Don Nelson said. "I like everything about him. He's a leader. He's honest. He has integrity. He has a wonderful family."

After he officially announced his retirement on January 31, 2000, the Mavericks brought their popular old point guard back as a vice president of business relations. He resigned after four months, but planned to stay in the basketball business.

"Throughout my career, I had a feel for what the business side was about," Harper said. "I have always looked at myself as someone who could make the transition from the basketball court to the business side. It's going to take a lot of work, but I'm willing to put forth the same effort I put forth as a player."

Curt Beamer, The News-Gazette

FROM LEFT, BOB HILTIBRAN, CHARLIE DUE AND BILL MITZE
DISCUSS A CALL DURING ILLINOIS' LOSS TO NO. 1 KENTUCKY.
THE THREE CAME OUT OF THE STANDS TO OFFICIATE WHEN
THE SCHEDULED REFS WERE UNABLE TO REACH TOWN.

Business Unusual

DECEMBER 24, 1983
BY LOREN TATE
NEWS-GAZETTE SPORTS EDITOR

CHAMPAIGN—Lou Henson aimed a frozen thunderbolt at college basketball's hierarchy Saturday and missed by the snap of a finger.

The underrated, unranked Illini grudgingly succumbed to No. 1 Kentucky's devastating 72-percent second-half shooting, freshman James Blackmon banking a hurried 12-footer to end it 56-54 with :01 on the Assembly Hall clock.

"I felt from the beginning that we could win," Henson said. "I told our players in the locker room that we are undefeated and Kentucky is undefeated, but it's our home court and we're supposed to win here. I genuinely felt we would, but Kentucky played a superior second half and we let down for eight or 10 minutes."

Blackmon's shot brought to an end an unusual contest played in the midst of sub-zero Midwest temperatures that limited the turnout to 7,651. The game was officiated by three former officials who came as spectators: Champaign Central baseball coach Charlie Due, UI agronomy professor Bob Hiltibran and Monticello principal Bill Mitze. The assigned officials were unable to reach Champaign because of the inclement weather.

Players and coaches on both sides lauded the refs for a fair and professional performance. The game was decided on the court by Kentucky's superior bench, Joe Hall receiving 15 points and eight rebounds from his reserves while the UI's lone sub, Tom Schafer, didn't score.

"This game should gain us some respect," Illinois' Doug Altenberger said. "I don't feel a lot of people believed in this team. That's why we felt so good when the 7,000 fans gave us a standing ovation at the end. I want to thank those who came out in this weather."

Altenberger, who was recruited by Kentucky out of Peoria Richwoods, scored a game-high 19 points.

"That's college basketball heaven," he said. "I wasn't sure I could play there with all those great athletes."

John Dixon, The News-Gazette

GEORGE MONTGOMERY, SHOOTING OVER TIM MCCORMICK, WAS POOPED AFTER ILLINOIS' FOUR-OVERTIME 75-66 WIN AGAINST MICHIGAN. THE WIN WAS LOU HENSON'S 399TH AS A COACH.

Marathon Men

JANUARY 28, 1984
BY LOREN TATE
NEWS-GAZETTE SPORTS EDITOR

CHAMPAIGN—George Montgomery, the structural glue holding the arms and legs of this "iron man" quintet together, flopped his hulking body in a chair with scarred knees angled outward, his head flopping like a jack-out-of-the-box.

"Man," he whispered, barely audible. "That was scary. I'm just gonna relax tonight. Nothing strenuous. That was really physical."

Doug Altenberger, battered from being knocked to the court a half-dozen times, once requiring medical assistance, nodded in agreement.

"I kept telling myself we weren't gonna lose, even if it took eight overtimes," he said. "Lou (Henson) kept trying something different at the start of each overtime, trying to fire us up.

"Finally he just said, 'This is our home court. Let's run the offense and take it to them. Let's be aggressive.'"

And in a record-breaking fourth overtime, with all five Illinois starters puffing through at least 51 of the 60 tension-packed minutes, with the crowd of 15,952 beginning to lose its collective voice, the Illini broke ahead on a jumper by Quinn Richardson and actually wore down the bigger, deeper Michigan Wolverines 75-66.

This 399th career win for Henson—exuberant boosters carried him off the court—lifted Illinois to 15-2 overall, assuring further ascension among the nation's top 10, and 6-1 in the Big Ten to remain deadlocked with Purdue for the lead.

Efrem Winters scored 23 points and three other starters reached double figures for the Illini.

"This is one of the greatest wins I've ever been associated with," Henson said. "I think we won on courage and determination."

Winters, who scored 15 of his points in the first half, wasn't sure how long the game went, guessing, "Four overtimes, I think."

Henson came to his rescue. "That's OK," he said before a swarm of reporters. "I didn't remember either."

AN INJURED ANKLE KEPT EFREM WINTERS (24) FROM PLAYING AT FULL STRENGTH IN THE ILLINI'S NCAA TOURNAMENT LOSS TO KENTUCKY. WINTERS HAD SEVEN POINTS IN THE ELITE EIGHT GAME.

Bump in the Road

MARCH 24, 1984
BY LOREN TATE
NEWS-GAZETTE SPORTS EDITOR

LEXINGTON, Ky.—The yellow brick road to the Final Four in Seattle is not paved with moral victories, and that was Illinois' empty reward for a Herculean effort in the Baron's cavern Saturday.

Moments after upset sensation Indiana lost a last-minute thriller to Virginia in Atlanta, Lou Henson's Illini piled up respect but came up short 54-51 in an NCAA tournament dogfight with tall, talented Kentucky in Rupp Arena.

"Our guys played a courageous game," Henson said, "and with just a break here or there, we could be in the Final Four in Seattle. We played tough defense, stopped their break and took no bad shots, but we could never gain control because the shots didn't fall when we needed them to.

"Kentucky is too strong at home to beat with below-par shooting."

Reminding of a football afternoon at Ohio State when David Wilson and the Illini were cheered in defeat (49-42), these Southern connoisseurs of smooth bourbon, fast horses and winning basketball cascaded praise toward the losers' side for a job well done.

But Kentucky, a giant in the sport since Adolph Rupp walked onto the campus a half-century ago, extended its marvelous tradition by advancing out of the Midwest Regional in quest of its sixth NCAA title and first since 1978.

"I'd like to compliment the Illini," Kentucky coach Joe B. Hall said. "They would certainly have been excellent representatives in Seattle. Their defense was awesome . . . and we exhausted a lot of options to find a way to score."

Quinn Richardson scored 16 points and Doug Altenberger had 13 for the Illini, who got 11 assists from Bruce Douglas. Efrem Winters, playing with a sore, heavily taped ankle, had seven points.

"Efrem did all right, although I don't believe his game statistics are indicative of how well he can play," Henson said. "Under the circumstances, we're proud of his effort."

IN 1984, BRUCE DOUGLAS HELPED ILLI-
NOIS TO ITS FIRST BIG TEN TITLE IN 21 YEARS.
THE HEADY POINT GUARD LED THE TEAM IN AS-
SISTS ALL FOUR YEARS HE PLAYED.

BRUCE DOUGLAS

GOOD HANDS MAN

BY JEFF D'ALESSIO

Bruce Douglas' 765 assists held up as the Big Ten record for nearly 15 years. Could have been 50 if the conference hadn't had such sticklers for statisticians in those days.

"When I played, an assist really was an assist," Douglas said. "Today, an assist is if you throw it and the dude makes three moves and gets a basket. Back then, you really had to assist in a basket. Especially on the road."

Douglas never expected his career assists record to last as long as it did. Nor did he expect it to fall in 2000, the year Michigan State All-American Mateen Cleaves snatched it from him.

The day before Cleaves did it, Douglas got a call from an old college buddy who let him know he was in danger of being passed. All Cleaves needed to break the record was 16 assists. But all the Spartans had left on the Big Ten schedule was one home game, against rival Michigan.

"I said, 'Oh, he'll never get (16) assists,'" Douglas said. "That ain't going to happen. Not in a Big Ten game."

Guess again. The Spartans piled it on the Wolverines that day, scoring 114 points in their biggest rout of a national championship season. And Cleaves piled up a record 20 assists, breaking the record Douglas had set 14 years earlier.

Douglas, who took it from Purdue's Bruce Parkinson, didn't mind Cleaves taking it from him. Well, at least Bruce Douglas didn't mind. Other members of the Douglas clan weren't quite as understanding.

"We've got a plan," said Bruce's wife, Madge. "Our son, Bruce II, is going to go down to Illinois and he's going to get it back."

The assists record wasn't the one Bruce was proudest of, anyway. And it's not his still-standing Big Ten career steals record (324), either.

No, the only one that Douglas will be a little sad about if it's ever broken is his endurance record at Illinois. In 130 games, including 117 starts, he put in 4,373 minutes—340 more than

BEFORE STARRING AT ILLINOIS, **BRUCE DOUGLAS** WAS A HIGH SCHOOL LEGEND, HELPING QUINCY HIGH BECOME A STATE POWERHOUSE AND MAKING THE McDONALD'S ALL-AMERICAN GAME, PUT ON BY JOHN WOODEN, RIGHT.

Photo courtesy of Bruce Douglas

the next guy on the list (ex-teammate Efrem Winters).

"I attribute all the assists and steals to conditioning," Douglas said. "Surely, smarts and the way you play the game have a lot to do with it, but I always thought that being in the best condition was probably the greatest advantage I always had. Mentally, I thought that physically I was better than anybody else."

Lou Henson's whole 1983-84 Big Ten championship team was that way, thanks in part to a rigorous conditioning program put in place by former strength coach Bill Kroll.

After home games, the players used to jog over to Memorial Stadium in the freezing cold and do a quick 20-minute circuit on the weights. It was the part of the day Douglas looked forward to the most.

He only remembers taking one night off. That happened on January 28, 1984, when Douglas was too drained to lift his own arms let alone a dumbbell.

Illinois beat Michigan 75-66 in four overtimes that day at the Assembly Hall and Douglas, the team's sophomore point guard, played all 60 minutes, a school record that appears as untouchable as Dave Downey's 53-point day.

It was one of many memorable moments during a thrill-filled 1984, the year the Illini brought home their first Big Ten title in 21 years. Their next time out, they won at Iowa in two overtimes. They beat Wisconsin on the road in overtime. They nipped Maryland 72-70 to advance to the Elite Eight.

Then they ran into Kentucky. At Kentucky. NCAA rules don't allow teams to play NCAA games on their home floors now, but it was OK back then. The Wildcats won that one 54-51, thanks to what some say was home cookin' by the refs.

"We were a basket away from the Final Four," Douglas said. "You can't play somebody in that kind of game on their court. You just can't do it at that level. You could just see how

the 20,000 people changed the referees' reactions on calls.

"We didn't lose because of refereeing. They played well enough to beat us. But you don't want to be put in that position, where you're playing to go to a Final Four and you're playing somebody on their homecourt. Especially Kentucky."

The Illini went on to win 26 games in Douglas' junior year and 22 more his senior season, making him 95-35 as an Illini. Winning was all it was ever about with Douglas, who led Quincy to 64 of them in a row during a glittery prep career.

"He didn't care who got the credit, as long as we won," former Illinois assistant Jimmy Collins said. "He was a very, very unselfish player. There wasn't all the flash and all that. He just played."

Oh, he'd throw an occasional alley-oop, but nothing too crazy. Douglas was more fundamental than flashy, the way Henson liked his point guards.

"I threw a lot of lobs, but not too many where I bounced them off my foot and kicked it up in the air, the stuff they do today," Douglas said. "Shoot, Lou would sit us down for that kind of stuff, man. He didn't even like the behind-the-back pass. I remember doing that in practice one time. He said, 'Hey, you're not in Hollywood. That won't work in the Big Ten.' So I stayed pretty basic."

He's as good a leader these days as he was in those days, only now it's a congregation instead of a basketball team he's in charge of. When he's not at Commonwealth Edison, where he works as a call center supervisor, you can usually find the happily married father of four at the Broadview Missionary Baptist Church in the Chicago suburbs, where he's an associate minister.

He preaches, teaches, counsels married couples and oversees the church's Youth Vacation Bible School.

"It's been a good life," Douglas said. "I can't complain."

DOUG ALTENBERGER DRIVES FOR TWO
OF HIS 20 POINTS IN THE ILLINI'S NATIONALLY
TELEVISED 69-67 WIN OVER INDIANA. IT WAS
ALTENBERGER'S LAST HOME GAME.

FIGHTING ILLINI
BASKETBALL
A HARDWOOD HISTORY

By JEFF D'ALESSIO

To this day, Kenny Battle still gets questions about the Battle to Seattle when he's touring the world with the Harlem Globetrotters.

Kendall Gill still catches flak from the Michigan guys whenever their NBA paths cross.

And shivers still run up Stephen Bardo's spine when he thinks back to the welcome-home party Illinois fans threw for him and the guys following the Final Four.

"I remember it all like it was yesterday," Gill said.

Hard to believe, but it's been more than a decade since Lou Henson's rim-rattling, alley-ooping Flyin' Illini reported for preseason practice.

You remember them. Nick. Stephen. Kenny. P.J. Kendall. Lowell. Andy. Marcus. Ervin. Larry.

"You're starting to get me excited again," former ticket manager Paul Bunting said.

A decade later, they still can rattle off the names and games in bars and barbershops from Buckley to Broadlands.

"You get a team like that, and they just become a part of you," said Orville Holman, the president of the Rebounders Club at the time.

"It's *your* team. *Our* guys. The terminology was altogether different when you talked to people."

Twenty years from now, they'll probably still be talking about Nick Anderson's 30-foot buzzer-beater in Bloomington, Battle's 360 dunks and the most popular team ever to wear orange and blue.

Sorry, '85 Bears.

"People loved that team," Henson said. "It was one of those teams that comes along every 25 or 30 or 40 years. We've had some good

teams, but I've never had a team that people enjoyed watching play as much as that one."

DIPSY DOO DUNKEROO

He nicknamed them. He praised them. He never saw anything quite like them.

Take it away, Dick Vitale.

basketball, making a fashion statement with their Bermuda shorts.

"Far be it for me to criticize anyone's dress, but I just remember them looking like ragamuffins," former Ball State coach Rick Majerus said.

And the next thing he knew, all of his players wanted a pair.

"I was involved with equipment, and the next year we had 20 or 30 schools call us up, asking, 'Where did you buy the shorts?'" assistant coach Mark Coomes said. "We changed the style of clothes."

Their cool threads weren't all that was unique about them.

They were all from the Land of Lincoln. They were all around the same size, no starter standing taller than 6-foot-6. And they could all jump like Jordan.

"Running, jumping and dunking—that's all we did, man," Larry Smith said.

FIGHTING ILLINI
BASKETBALL
A HARDWOOD HISTORY

"One of the most exciting groups I've ever watched play. I was absolutely thrilled on the sidelines watching them perform. Kendall Gill was absolutely sparkling, Stephen Bardo was a tremendous floor leader, Kenny Battle was a high riser. Lou-Do had that place rocking and rolling. It was showtime, baby. They were absolutely sensational. They didn't have the big aircraft carrier, but what they had was tremendous speed.

"I mean, they were reminiscent of the doctors of dunk—Louisville's

club in 1980—with a little slam, jam, bam. The pressure defense, the transition game and the high-rising ability that they had with those athletes was really unique and very special. It was awesome, BAY-BEE, with a capital A, to watch the Flyin' Illini do their thing. I mean, they were poetry in motion. They were Baryshnikov in shorts."

Yeah, baggy ones. They were the Tommy Hilfigers of college

"We had our little plays, but for the most part, we'd get after you on defense, use our long arms to steal the ball from you and throw an alley-oop."

They ripped off 341 steals—a school record by 31. They threw down 171 dunks—and looked good doing it.

"Any possible attempt at a dunk was made," said Eddie Manzke, a former walk-on. "The layups were very few that season."

Who can ever forget Battle's in-your-face, over-you-chump dunk on Dennis Scott in the Georgia Tech win?

Or Gill's backboard-shaking tomahawk against Syracuse in Minneapolis?

Or Lowell Hamilton's one-handed jam on Senior Day in Ann Arbor?

"You had spectacular players that could do spectacular things," P.J. Bowman said. "Not only were people into the pace of the game, but you

really had a sense of 'When is Kenny Battle going to get that next dunk?' or 'When is Kendall going to fly through the lane?' or 'When's there going to be another alley-oop to Lowell Hamilton?'

"We kept people on the edge of their seats."

LOOK WHO'S TALKING

"Memory escapes me momentarily," Bob Knight said. "Did they win the NCAA?"

Ooh, low blow.

Knight thought their coach was underrated, their guards were good and their defense was better than anything Schwarzkopf ever had.

But don't go comparing the Flyin' Illini to Indiana '76, Michigan '89 or Michigan State '00. At least not around "The General."

"How many teams have won the NCAA out of the Big Ten?" the Indiana coach asked.

Nine.

"How many teams have gone to the Final Four out of the Big Ten?

Thirty-eight.

"You're talking about a very good team, but I don't think you can go any further than that with it. I thought they would win the NCAA. But I'll tell you what I thought hurt them the most. If I remember correctly, they played Michigan the last game of the year and won easily (89-73 in Ann Arbor). Then, when they had to turn around and play Michigan again in the NCAA, that's always a tough kind of game, given the results of the previous game. I think without that particular matchup, Illinois might very well have won the NCAA."

It must have been a special team. Knight, who rarely grants interviews, returned a call to an out-of-town reporter to talk about it.

THE PEOPLE'S CHOICE

He's old enough to remember the Whiz Kids, the '52 Final Four gang and Harry Combes the player.

But former State Appellate Court Judge Fred Green, who has watched Illinois basketball games since 1933, would rule in favor of the Flyin' Illini in any greatest UI team of all time debate.

"That probably would have to be the best Illinois has ever had," Dike Eddleman's former teammate said.

No Illinois basketball team got off to a faster start than the Flyin' Illini, who ripped off 17 wins in a row to start the season.

No Illinois basketball team could fall so far behind and come so far back as the Flyin' Illini, who spotted Missouri 18, Georgia Tech 16 and Indiana 13—and won.

No Illinois basketball team put up more points than the Flyin' Illini, who broke 100 eight times, including a school-record 127 in a road romp over LSU.

FIGHTING ILLINI
BASKETBALL

"I thought it was the best team we ever played in Baton Rouge," said Dale Brown, LSU's coach for 25 years. "And we played a very tough schedule—the North Carolinas and UCLAs and Arizonas and UNLVs. They were just fun to watch. They were all jumping jacks. They all looked like they came out of a cloning machine or something."

They nabbed the school's first No. 1 ranking in 36 years, got invited to their first Final Four in 37.

So they didn't win the national title.

Or the Big Ten.

Name another team that had 13,000-plus fans waiting for them at the Assembly Hall when they got back from a loss.

"We were the kings," Gill said. "Even the football players gave us the ultimate respect back in those days. The professors loved us. Everybody got behind that team."

No Illinois basketball team created quite the ruckus in Campustown that Battle & Co. did, either.

From bumper stickers to "Lou Can Do" T-shirts, their stuff sold quicker than vendors could put it on the shelves.

"Everyone wanted to get on the bandwagon," said Gery Maury, whose sales at Gery & Al's Sporting Goods were 50 percent better that year than most others.

Everywhere the players went, there was a hand to shake, an autograph to sign, a baby to kiss.

Like being a Bull, Hamilton said.

"There wasn't a place in Champaign that we could go and not be recognized," Battle said.

Not even the classroom was safe. It got so bad in the few days between the win over Syracuse in Minneapolis and the takeoff for Seattle, some players blew off school for a few days.

"You'd get to class, and you'd get mobbed," Bardo said. "By the students, by the faculty. Media were trying to slip in. I remember saying, 'I'm not going to class. I'll pick up when we get back.' I couldn't deal with it."

It wasn't just Campustown. Or Champaign-Urbana. Or Illinois. Or the Midwest. They were America's team.

"I have people come up to me all the time and say, 'I had money bet on you guys in the tournament. That team was great,'" Gill said. "I could be in California, I could be in New York, I could be down in Florida. Even Japan, when I was there.

"I don't know how many teams that didn't win it have so many fans."

Seeing Red

MARCH 1, 1987
BY LOREN TATE
NEWS-GAZETTE SPORTS EDITOR

CHAMPAIGN—Picture 16,000 orange pompons all being waved in one frantic, full-circle display for the ABC cameras.

Picture Indiana's Bob Knight surrounded by his squad in a double-timeout huddle at :39, and daring to run the clock down with his team behind 69-67 and gamble for the win from three-point range.

Picture Lou Henson's long-frustrated athletes jumping for joy as Steve Bardo, after missing a free throw at :04, blocked Steve Alford's last-second heave from midcourt to end a spell of five narrow losses against the Big Ten's big three.

That's what a Sunday afternoon at the Assembly Hall provided, a picturesque and motivating Illini crowd yelling itself hoarse in yet another heart-stopping finishing in which the 14th-ranked Illini prevailed 69-67 over No. 3 Indiana.

Illinois improved to 21-7 overall with Big Ten games left at Michigan and Michigan State. A split would virtually assure the Illini of a top 16 seed in the NCAA tournament.

Ken Norman bagged 24 points, Doug Altenberger had 20 and Tony Wysinger added 10 in the seniors' final home game.

"It was nice to win the last home game for the three seniors, but I'm not so sure we haven't had better opportunities to win other games than we did this one," said Henson, noting his team's five previous Big Ten losses were by a total of 13 points, three in overtime. "The seniors deserve most of the credit, but let's not forget the four big points by (Jens) Kujawa and the all-around play of Bardo.

"We are a different team now than we were in December because of those two. We're better defensively and we're better on the boards."

Kujawa's hook and two free throws put the Illini ahead 69-65 with 1:47 left. Bardo kept Ricky Calloway to eight points on 2-of-7 shooting and chipped in seven rebounds, seven assists, five points, three blocks and three steals. And Altenberger got the best of Alford, holding him to 6-of-16 shooting while making six three-pointers himself.

THE ILLINI'S UPSET LOSS TO AUSTIN PEAY IN
THE FIRST ROUND OF THE NCAA TOURNAMENT
WAS SEALED WHEN KEN NORMAN MISSED
A JUMP SHOT OUTSIDE THE FREE THROW LINE
AT THE BUZZER.

March Sadness

MARCH 12, 1987
BY LOREN TATE
NEWS-GAZETTE SPORTS EDITOR

BIRMINGHAM, Ala.—Last March the NCAA's embarrassed first-round losers were Indiana and Notre Dame, to this day living down upset losses to Cleveland State and Arkansas-Little Rock.

This year it's third-seeded Illinois and Big Eight champion Missouri. They realized their worst fears Thursday as victims of unexpected one-point losses to underdogs Austin Peay and Xavier.

Tony Raye, a regular who averaged just three field goal attempts this season and attempted none in 33 minutes Thursday, deposited two free throws at :02 to eliminate the snake-bit Illini 68-67.

UI second-team All-American Ken Norman got off a jumper from just outside the free throw line at the buzzer but it was off line, leaving Lou Henson's athletes with their eighth loss, seven of them by a total of 15 points and all imminently winnable.

"Wouldn't you know it would end this way?" fumed Henson. "Our young players reverted to form and we didn't shoot it the way we can, either from the field or the free throw line."

Said Norman: "I had a chance to be a hero. It was a good shot, but some go in and some don't. I have to share the blame."

The Illini trailed most of the second half, fighting back from a 49-42 deficit to squeeze ahead 56-55 and 60-59. The game remained close until the final buzzer.

"First, we'd like to thank Paul Finebaum of the *Birmingham Post-Herald* for writing that we'd be 'no trouble' and Dick Vitale of ESPN for saying we have a 'matador defense,'" Austin Peay coach Lake Kelly said. "I guess Dick still doesn't have his eye in right.

"Tonight at halftime, when the score was tied, he said he'd stand upside down on the table if Austin Peay defeated Illinois. That's what he wound up doing, standing upside down on the table. Maybe that got his brains back up in there where they belong."

The News-Gazette Archives

STEPHEN BARDO, LEFT, LOVED PLAY-
ING MISSOURI IN THE BORDER WAR. THE
CARBONDALE NATIVE WENT 4-0 AGAINST
MISSOURI IN HIS TIME AT ILLINOIS.

One for the Border

DECEMBER 19, 1988
BY LOREN TATE
NEWS-GAZETTE SPORTS EDITOR

S T. LOUIS—Lou Henson's Fighting Illini passed their first major test the hard way Monday night.

Down by 18 points with 4:05 left in the first half, they caught up in an electric seven-minute span and defeated rugged Missouri 87-84.

With pressure thick as steam from an overheated radiator, the Illini converted 13 of their last 14 free throws and shot a blistering 65.5 percent from the field in the second half.

Kenny Battle, who led the furious charge with 28 points, put the UI ahead 85-84 with two free ones following a timeout at :26, then deflected a deep Tiger pass to get the ball back.

"He certainly has the right last name," Missouri coach Norm Stewart said of Battle.

Larry Smith iced it with a reverse layup at :04.

The bitterly fought contest, played before a sellout St. Louis Arena crowd of 18,561, was Illinois' sixth straight win against Missouri, the fifth-ranked Illini improving to 8-0.

"You learn a lot in a game like this," said Illini Nick Anderson, who had eight points and a game-high 10 rebounds. "We needed a tough game, and we fought to the end. We took Kenny as our leader because he plays hard all the time. It rubs off."

Lowell Hamilton scored 21 points and Kendall Gill added 11 as Illinois held off several late Missouri charges.

Battle called the second half "one of my best," adding:

"I'm a senior and I'm supposed to pick the other guys up. I tried to stay aggressive."

It was the UI's first game not at home this season.

"This win could help us, knowing that we can come back from that distance against such a good team," Henson said. "This should help our confidence. I think we realize that we didn't really play that well.

"We got in foul trouble and we made too many mistakes, but we gave a great effort. And we made our free throws. That's how you win close games. When you miss them, you lose. It's that simple."

KENNY BATTLE, THE MOST POPULAR
OF THE FLYIN' ILLINI, IS STILL IN HEAVY
DEMAND TODAY. WHEN HE RETURNED TO
CAMPUS IN THE SUMMER OF 2000, HE WAS
GREETED WITH A STANDING OVATION.

KENNY BATTLE

FLIGHT 33

BY JEFF D'ALESSIO

Believe it or not, Kenny Battle isn't the most popular Illinois basketball player of all time.

That honor still belongs to the only guy to run in a Rose Bowl, jump in the Olympics and dribble in a Final Four, a recent *News-Gazette* reader survey showed.

But in the 50 years A.D. (After Dike), no Illini has wowed the crowd quite like the highest-flyin' of the Flyin' Illini.

Said Mr. Billy Packer, sportscaster, New York:

"Kenny Battle was one of those guys that the NBA doesn't have enough of but was the perfect college player. It's unfortunate the NBA doesn't have room for that type of player because you'd pay to watch him play."

Said Sergio McClain, 21, Champaign:

"He reminded me of me, man. Hard-nosed, did whatever it took to win. Just a warrior."

Said Mr. Steve Fisher, basketball coach, San Diego:

"He didn't appear to have a huge ego, where he had to be the brightest star. But despite all the great players they had, he might have been."

Said Andy Kaufmann, residence care worker, Jacksonville:

"Kenny was the Michael Jordan of Illinois basketball that year. He was Mr. Popularity. He was the man. People came to see Kenny."

GRAND SLAM

For our next survey, maybe we'll hit on a new topic.

Favorite Kenny Battle dunk.

Now there's a way to stir up a debate.

"The one I remember more than any of Battle's was at Ohio State," former Illinois assistant Mark Coomes said. "He got an offensive rebound, and Grady Mateen at 6-foot-11 was between him and the basket. And Battle took one step and dunked the ball behind his head over the top

John Dixon, The News-Gazette

LIKE DIKE EDDLEMAN, KENNY BATTLE HAS AN
AWARD NAMED AFTER HIM AT HIS ALMA MATER. HIS
HONORS HUSTLE AND GRIT.

of Grady Mateen for a three-point play. Now that was incredible."

You want incredible? You should have seen Battle in March 1988 at Northwestern. Eleven seconds left. Lou Henson's Illini up three. Play-it-safe time.

"It was a very close game, and he had a wide-open layup," Henson said. "But instead of laying it in, he did a 360! We could have lost the game. He made the dunk, but we don't like 360s at the end of close ballgames."

That was No. 33 for you. Always the showman.

"Human highlight film, man," former teammate Larry Smith said.

"You should have seen the stuff he'd do in practice," Stephen Bardo said. "You would have just run out of the gym, you wouldn't have even believed it."

Everyone has a favorite Battle jam. Including Battle.

"Probably the dunk against Florida," he said. "It was an out-of-bounds play right in front of our bench. Larry Smith threw a lob from out of bounds, and I caught it on top of one of the Florida guys."

Kaboom.

"He was as good an athlete as anybody that Michigan's Fab Five had," former Wisconsin coach Steve Yoder said.

"Oh, man, I've seen him dunk over many 7-footers," Lowell Hamilton said. "And he looked good doing it. Nick Anderson was power. Kenny Battle was power and finesse at the same time."

Topping Ted Beach's list: Battle's reverse slam in the second Georgia Tech game.

"That one would do Michael Jordan proud," the UI's official timer said.

Rod Cardinal, the UI's trainer, would cast his vote for Battle's blind double-pump reverse layup in the Syracuse game. Beats any of the dunks as far as he's concerned.

"He was at one side of the basket. You blinked. He was at the other side of the basket. You blinked again. And he was underneath the basket, in the lane, flipping it up," Cardinal said. "I don't know how he did that. I mean, I look at that Syracuse tape every once in awhile, and I still don't know how he did that play."

THE HUSTLER

Pardon Henson, who hasn't kept up on his Illini postseason awards since leaving for New Mexico State.

"Do they still give out the Kenny Battle Award?" he asked.

Sure do.

"Oh, that's good," he said.

Along with the Final Four flag hanging from the rafters at the Assembly Hall, it's one of the few mementos left over from the Flyin' Illini.

Each year, the Kenny Battle Inspirational Award goes to the guy who shows the most spunk, tracks down the most loose balls, wins the most suicide sprints after practice.

A Nate Mast. A Brian Johnson. A Tom Michael.

"A hustle award," Hamilton said. "Very appropriate."

Graduate assistant Scott Nagy never has come across a guy who got after it like the tire-less Battle, who more than one ex-teammate said should be doing commercials for Energizer.

"He was like the bunny: always moving," former assistant Dick Nagy said. "Wouldn't let you lose."

He was the only Illini on top of his game in Seattle with 29 points and seven rebounds against Michigan. He had 28 on a gimpy knee against Syracuse in Minneapolis. As a senior, he won the Border War all by his lonesome, came up with 25 big ones against Georgia Tech and averaged 23 in three games against the national champs.

"Is there such a word as 'emotionalize'?" Bardo asked. "Kenny gave emotion to what our team was all about. Very fiery. Nick Anderson was very competitive, but he was very, very quiet. Kendall (6-11) was very stoic. I'm kind of outwardly (energetic) but not as much as Kenny Battle. He was the spirit of that team."

He didn't have the best jumper of the Flyin' Illini, but he was their top shooter and second-leading scorer. He's No. 28 on Illinois' all-time scoring list, even though he spent his first two years at Northern Illinois, and No. 3 all time in field goal percentage.

So what if half his baskets were tips and tomahawks.

"I remember the managers could beat him in a game of H-O-R-S-E," Kaufmann said. "He couldn't shoot it. I never saw him really work on his shooting. He didn't have to. He got by with dunks and little flip shots. His jumper wasn't there, but he had everything else."

Bardo won the Big Ten's Defensive Player of the Year Award in 1989, but Battle could have made a case. His 89 steals that season are still the most in Illinois history. His 72 the year before are the most by anyone not named Bruce Douglas.

"Kenny could guard a whole team by himself almost," Ervin Small said. "As fast as the ball could be passed, I believe he could get to it."

FROM **P.J. BOWMAN** TO THE WALK-ONS, EVERYONE GOT IN THE ACT FOR ILLINOIS IN ITS SCHOOL RECORD-SETTING ROMP OVER LSU. THE ILLINI MADE 68 PERCENT OF THEIR SHOTS FOR 127 POINTS.

Bayou Blowout

DECEMBER 22, 1988
BY LOREN TATE
NEWS-GAZETTE SPORTS EDITOR

BATON ROUGE, La.—Look out Hawaii, here comes red-hot Illinois.
Lou Henson's dashing, dunking mini-machine, breaking records left and right, shattered the defense and broke the spirit of LSU's proud Tigers on Thursday.

By winning 127-100, the Illini broke the school record of 126 points against Long Island in 1982, tied the all-time mark for most Illini field goals (53) and ran up the most points by a Louisiana State opponent in Pete Maravich Assembly Center. It also broke the UI record of 220 set in 1977 for most points scored in a game by both teams.

"Lou Henson has some thoroughbreds . . . that's the finest group of athletes I've ever seen in this building," LSU's 17th-year coach Dale Brown said. "That's got to be a shooting record. If not, I don't know who has shot better."

The Illini were shooting 73.3 percent from the field—24 of their first 38 baskets were dunks or layups—when Henson began clearing the bench with 7 1/2 minutes to go. They finished at 67.9 percent, just below the UI record of 69.1

The ninth consecutive win created Illinois' longest season-opening win streak since 1979 when the Illini won their first 15. They're averaging 99.7 points, have topped 100 four times and would have hit triple figures in three others if Henson had not pulled the plug. Henson's seven "starters" are shooting 56.7 percent on three-pointers as they leave for Honolulu on Friday.

"Illinois doesn't have a big man but everybody is big," Brown said. "That's a Final Four team. The only way we could win was by keeping them from getting inside. When they started hitting outside, that was it."

Kendall Gill drilled a personal-high 27 points, Lowell Hamilton had 24, Kenny Battle notched 17 and Nick Anderson offered 16 points and 12 rebounds.

"This is the first time I've felt like a failure," Brown said. "I believe we thought they were better and we couldn't beat them, and we just gave up."

KENNY BATTLE SIGNALS WHERE ILLINOIS STANDS IN THE POLLS AFTER ITS 103-92 NAIL-BITER AGAINST GEORGIA TECH ON SUPER BOWL SUNDAY. KENDALL GILL'S INJURY WOULD MAKE IT A SHORT STAY AT THE TOP.

John Dixon, The News-Gazette

Who's No. 1?

JANUARY 22, 1989
BY LOREN TATE
NEWS-GAZETTE SPORTS EDITOR

C HAMPAIGN—The University of Illinois waited 36 years, 952 games and two overtimes for one sunshiny afternoon in January 1989.

Sharing the excitement of a Super Bowl Sunday, the Illini rallied from 16 points down to defeat Georgia Tech 103-92 in 50 intense minutes of basketball amid the bedlam of the Assembly Hall.

The lone unbeaten Division I team in the country, Illinois has won a school-record 17 consecutive games and will be recognized as the nation's No. 1 team for the first time since 1953.

But the sun hadn't set on a day of celebration before the 17-0 Illini received a devastating blow to their Big Ten hopes. The X-ray report from the hospital indicated junior guard Kendall Gill, who limped off at the start of the first overtime, sustained a stress fracture in his foot. He underwent surgery and a pin was placed in his foot. He has been ruled out 7-8 weeks, which means he probably won't participate in the remaining 14 conference games.

"It's nice for the players, the school and the fans for us to be No. 1, but I'm still thinking about what we have to face in the immediate future," UI coach Lou Henson said. "Duke was No. 1 and you saw how quickly they lost two games. For me, it just means that much more work."

Whatever the future brings, Sunday remains one of the high points in Illini athletics. The UI trailed 47-31 before rallying.

"Our guys put a lot into this game, but what else is new?" Henson said. "They've been doing that all season. Tech almost gave us the knockout punch, but we hung in there."

Kenny Battle scored 25 points and the other four starters reached double figures. Gill had 19 points before leaving the game. With a minute left, fans began chanting "We're No. 1, We're No. 1."

"We felt if we got the defense going, the offense would catch up," Battle said. "We try to come out strong every game but we were flat in this one, and it took us awhile to get going."

Robert K. O'Daniell, The News-Gazette

NICK ANDERSON REACTS AFTER BURYING A
GAME-WINNING SHOT AGAINST INDIANA. THE IM-
PROBABLE JUMPER TYPIFIED THE FLYIN' ILLINI'S
IMPROBABLE RUN TO THE FINAL FOUR.

The Shot

MARCH 5, 1989
BY LOREN TATE
NEWS-GAZETTE SPORTS EDITOR

BLOOMINGTON, Ind.—"This just proves . . . once again . . . that you can never give up."

This was Illini coach Lou Henson's first comment after leaving an Indiana basketball court that changed suddenly from a body-strewn battlefield to the site of an Illini victory pileup.

Nick Anderson salvaged a 70-67 triumph with a shocking 30-foot buzzer beater that followed a tying jumper by Indiana's Jay Edwards at :02. It was Illinois' fourth straight victory, seventh in eight Big Ten games and the third in a row against Indiana.

Edwards' improbable 17-footer lifted Indiana into a 67-67 tie. The clock ran out but official Ed Hightower dashed to the scorer's table to put time back on it.

"I could see it was going in," Illinois guard Steve Bardo said, "and I was close enough to Mr. Hightower to get his attention. We both had a clear view of the clock."

Meanwhile, coach Lou Henson, who always seems to come up with the right play in these situations, came up with a strategy that Indiana did not anticipate.

Indiana sent no one to challenge Bardo's long baseball peg and, strangely, double-teamed Larry Smith in the backcourt.

Said Anderson: "Coach told me to come out from behind Kenny (Battle) and Lowell (Hamilton), to use them as a screen and come out for the ball. He told me to take one bounce. That's what I did. I took one dribble and shot it. There was no time to do anything else."

It was Illinois' longest game-winning shot since Derek Harper drilled a three-point bomb to beat Minnesota in 1983.

"For me, it's never happened before and it'll probably never happen again," Anderson said. "This is the shot I'll always remember. I arched it, and it felt good when I got it off, but I didn't know until it neared the basket that it was going in.

"When it was coming down, I could see it falling. I could see it was good."

NICK ANDERSON

TWO YEARS TO REMEMBER

BY JEFF D'ALESSIO

The Flyin' Illini can't blame Nick Anderson for taking off after the 1988-89 season. But they also can't help but wonder what might have been had he returned for his senior year.

"I'm just sorry he left," Kendall Gill said. "Because if he hadn't left, we'd probably be talking about a national championship."

And maybe, just maybe, a No. 1 draft pick. Even though Anderson was taken in the lottery and signed a multimillion-dollar contract and went on to enjoy a long, prosperous NBA career, Lou Henson thought he could have done a lot better for himself had he stuck around for his senior season.

No doubt it would have been better for his alma mater, which stumbled against 12th-seeded Dayton the next year in a first-round NCAA game.

"Had he come back the next year, he would have scored 25 to 30 a game," Henson said. "He was that good. But we didn't need him to score because we had (Kenny) Battle and other people. If he came back, he would have gotten three or four times the money he did.

"I don't think NBA people knew how good he really was."

Henson knew. He knew from the first day he saw the 6-foot-6 Anderson playing small forward for Bob Hambric at Chicago's Simeon High that this was a one-of-a-kind talent Illinois had to have.

Henson just wished he could have coached him for more than two years. Anderson sat out his freshman season as a Proposition 48 casualty, then split after leading Illinois to its first Final Four in 37 years.

But he left behind plenty of memories. No. 1 in Illini fans' hearts: his 30-foot bomb at the buzzer to beat Bob Knight's Hoosiers in Bloomington. It was the play of the year in 1988-89, beating out any Battle dunk or Gill alley-oop.

For true orange and blue fans, it's the man-landing-on-the-moon of shots. More than a decade later, every one of them can tell you exactly where he was on March 5, 1989, right down to the fabric of the couch he was plopped down on.

"We had gone to a friend's house and . . . god, do you have to write this?" said Mike Smith, a high-strung Champaign accountant and longtime season ticket holder. "I couldn't stay in the room. During the timeout, I just couldn't stand it anymore, so I got up and walked out. Then I couldn't stand not being there, either, so I peeked around the corner at the TV. I couldn't go all the way in the room. I just peeked. But I did get to see the ball thrown to Nick and then him go up and shoot it and it go in and everybody just go bananas.

"God, isn't it amazing what you remember after 10 years? One shot?"

That's not all fans remember about Anderson in '89, the year he walked off with MVP honors at the Rainbow Classic, scored 35 at Ohio State and was so magnificent in Minneapolis, coming through with 48 points and 21 rebounds in NCAA thrillers against Louisville and Syracuse.

"I've never had a player who was better in the clutch," Henson said. "Never."

Anderson averaged 15.9 points as a sophomore and 18.0 as a junior, and ranks 20th on Illinois' all-time scoring list despite only putting in two years.

He played his next 10 for the Orlando Magic, who made him their first NBA draft pick. Anderson made them proud in return, setting all-time franchise records for points

The News-Gazette Archives

NICK ANDERSON IS ONE OF TWO FLYIN' ILLINI TO LAST MORE THAN 10 YEARS IN THE NBA. HIS CAREER HAS TAKEN HIM TO ORLANDO AND SACRAMENTO.

(10,650), field goals (4,075), steals (1,004) and games (692) before being shipped to Sacramento in August 1999.

All along, he's worn the same number—25—in honor of former Simeon teammate Ben Wilson, who was gunned down a block away from school on November 20, 1984. Anderson started the tradition of wearing Wilson's uniform number at Illinois, which fellow Simeon standouts Deon Thomas and Bryant Notree did later.

"Every time I put on my basketball uniform, I think of him," Anderson said.

NICK ANDERSON WALKED OFF WITH MIDWEST REGIONAL MVP HONORS AFTER HIS PERFORMANCE AGAINST LOUISVILLE AND SYRACUSE. ANDERSON WOULD LEAVE CAMPUS A MONTH LATER.

The Battle to Seattle

MARCH 26, 1989
BY LOREN TATE
NEWS-GAZETTE SPORTS EDITOR

MINNEAPOLIS—Two domes down and one to go.
The team with "something special" rode its intangibles to new heights before 33,496 fans in the Metrodome on Sunday. Defeating Syracuse 89-86, Lou Henson's Flying Illini attained the dream of every college basketball player, a berth in the Final Four.

It is Illinois' first venture into that elite circle since 1952.

Carried along with a cry of "Battle to Seattle," Henson's athletes came roaring from 13 points behind with a withering second-half assault. Illinois led throughout the last six minutes and Kenny Battle, who combined with Nick Anderson to score 52 points, iced the win with two free throws with 15 seconds left.

Moments later, this team of destiny was sprawled on the Metrodome court, alternately praying, hugging and inventing new rap songs for the milling throng.

"In 34 years of coaching, I've never seen a more gallant performance than these athletes gave up here," Henson said. "They just won't die. I thought Friday's win over Louisville, under the circumstances, was the greatest I'd seen. But this one was just like it. Kenny Battle was remarkable when you consider that couldn't even run on Friday."

Illinois survived the Louisville scare with both seniors, Battle and Lowell Hamilton, severely hobbled. Hamilton played sparingly Sunday on a sprained ankle, but Battle came back with a vengeance. A whirling dervish, he assaulted the 6-foot-9 Syracuse postmen, all 11 of his field goals coming within 7 feet of the basket. One blind, twisting flip by this muscular contortionist defied explanation.

"These two games were amazing," Henson said, "when you consider our injuries and the way we shot free throws (13 of 26 against Syracuse). But these guys hang together. They like each other and they've been brought even closer together because of all the adversity we've faced."

Anderson had a career-high 16 rebounds and was named Midwest Regional MVP. Battle and Kendall Gill also made the all-tournament team.

"Our goal now is simply to get everyone healthy for Seattle," Henson said.

LOWELL HAMILTON (45) MANEUVERS INSIDE AGAINST MICHIGAN'S LOY VAUGHT. HAMILTON WASN'T ON THE COURT FOR THE BITTER END OF THE NATIONAL SEMIFINAL, FOULING OUT IN THE CLOSING MINUTES.

Robert K. O'Daniell, The News-Gazette

Heartbreak Hotel

APRIL 1, 1989
BY LOREN TATE
NEWS-GAZETTE SPORTS EDITOR

SEATTLE—Third time was a charm for tall, talented Michigan.

Sean Higgins, a 6-foot-9 Californian, soared high over Illinois' smaller rebounders and punched home a short put-back at :02 to give the Wolverines an 83-81 triumph and a spot opposite Seton Hall in Monday night's NCAA title game at the Kingdome.

Illinois' quickness had prevailed over Michigan twice this season and six times in the last seven meetings, but the weight of Michigan's superior size, coupled with renewed dedication under interim coach Steve Fisher, prevailed in a semifinal shootout before 39,187 fans.

In the last five minutes, Michigan scored five baskets, all on the inside.

"If we could have cleared a few key rebounds, we could have won the game," Illinois coach Lou Henson said. "That's been a problem we've had to deal with all season."

Kenny Battle, who scored a game-high 29 points, tied it at 81 with a short-angle jumper at :30. Michigan held for the last shot but didn't get the one it wanted. Terry Mills' long corner jumper was off the mark but caromed to Higgins, who went back up with the point-blank winner. It broke the seventh tie in a game that had 33 lead changes.

"In the end, we defended them pretty well but we couldn't get the ball off the boards," Henson said.

It marked the end of a memorable season. The Illini won more games (31), scored more points (3,110), swiped more balls (341) and scored the most points in a single game (127 at LSU) than any team in school history.

"In the eyes of some, our team will go down as a pretty good team," Henson said, "but in my eyes, it will go down as a team that gave a great performance all season. This team won by outworking their opponents, but there was too much size, too much pushing and shoving, and we couldn't do it tonight."

Hard to Say Goodbye

MAY 14, 1989
BY LOREN TATE
NEWS-GAZETTE SPORTS EDITOR

CHAMPAIGN—The University of Illinois' dream of repeating its Final Four basketball foray in 1990 hit an unexpected snag this weekend.

Nick Anderson, 21-year-old Mr. Clutch for the 31-5 Flying Illini, made a stunning 11th-hour decision to leave school and turn pro.

Stopped by reporters at the Bulls-Knicks playoff game in Chicago on Saturday, Anderson explained that multiple injuries sustained by his mother, Alberta Anderson, in a January auto accident could make it impossible for her to continue to work.

"I'm in a situation where I can help my mom," he said. "I don't think anybody can fault you for trying to help your mother."

With Anderson sending his letter of application to the NBA, Illinois is without the mature, explosive front line that spearheaded the most fun-filled basketball season in modern times. Anderson, a junior, and Kenny Battle and Lowell Hamilton, both seniors, helped the UI win more games, play before more fans and earn more money than any team in UI history.

Anderson first informed assistant coach Jimmy Collins on Friday.

"We both passed some tears because I wanted him to stay, and he wants to stay, but circumstances surrounding his family are difficult," Collins said. "Nick is the only breadwinner in the family at this time."

Anderson led the Illini in scoring (18.0) and rebounding (7.9), was voted runner-up to Michigan's Glen Rice as Big Ten MVP and was a projected preseason All-American in 1989-90.

"This came as a total surprise," said UI coach Lou Henson, who was in Chicago for the weekend and as of Saturday still had not talked directly to Anderson.

Assistant coach Dick Nagy and Anderson spoke Saturday morning.

"Nick explained that it was a financial thing," he said. "He didn't want any bad feelings but he felt he had to do it. I had talked to him before and I had no inkling, none at all."

KENDALL GILL'S 20.0 SCORING AVERAGE IN 1989-90 RANKS NINTH BEST AMONG SENIOR SCORERS AT ILLINOIS. GILL IS THE UI'S LAST BIG TEN SCORING CHAMP.

Gill the Thrill

MARCH 11, 1990
BY LOREN TATE
NEWS-GAZETTE SPORTS EDITOR

BLOOMINGTON, Ind.—Sunday provided a storybook Big Ten finish for coach Lou Henson's gutty travelers.

Illinois defeated Indiana for the fifth straight time, 69-63, to tie Minnesota for fourth place at 11-7 . . . senior Kendall Gill racked 23 points to become the UI's first Big Ten scoring leader since Andy Phillip in 1943 . . . and Illinois drew an NCAA top 20 basketball berth opposite red-hot Dayton in Austin, Texas.

Cheers reverberated on the bus heading for home as the NCAA pairings came via battery-operated TV sets.

"It's great to go into the tournament off a road victory," Henson said, "although that doesn't always assure that you'll play well the next time out. But this was very satisfying and it shows we can win on the road."

Henson tied Harry Combes for most coaching wins at Illinois at 316. And Gill beat Minnesota's Willie Burton for the scoring title, finishing with two free throws with six seconds left.

"I'm glad for Kendall," Henson said. "He's done a lot for this basketball program."

Gill found out he won the scoring title from his dad, who was seated courtside and relayed the news through P.J. Bowman.

"More than anything, the win is what I'm proud of," Gill said. "As for the scoring title, I'm proud to be so fortunate. Coach Henson gave me the chance, and he said to let them foul me in the final seconds.

"I wasn't sure whether the first free throw would go through, but as it got closer I saw it would be good. It's a big thrill."

After the game, Indiana coach Bob Knight drew catcalls of "cheap shot" and "no class" from Illinois fans for his Senior Day remarks. He expressed disappointment in Sunday's outcome, then noted to the pleasure of the assemblage that, at least, Indiana's program "is not under investigation."

Illinois received an NCAA official inquiry February 22.

KENDALL GILL WAS ONE OF THREE IL-
LINOIS GUARDS TO BE NAMED ALL-BIG TEN
IN THE 1990S. KIWANE GARRIS (1996, '97)
AND KEVIN TURNER (1998) ALSO MADE THE
ALL-CONFERENCE CUT.

KENDALL GILL

FROM ANONYMOUS TO ALL-STAR

BY JEFF D'ALESSIO

E rvin Small didn't need an alarm clock his last year at Illinois.

He had Kendall Gill.

"Every morning, I'd wake up to the sound of 'clink, clink, clink,'" Small said. "It'd be Kendall lifting those weights."

Oscar Madison was Roommate of the Year compared to the Flyin' Illini's fitness fanatic. Living with Gill took more out of Small than the games themselves.

"He used to have a little thing when we were watching TV. Every time a commercial came on, we'd see who could do the most pushups," Small said. "Or the most situps. Who could do the most situps while the commercials were on?"

And you didn't want to be anywhere near Gill when Michael Jordan and the Bulls were on.

"That guy had us watching Chicago Bulls games on film all night," Small said. "He'd be like, 'Hold on, hold on. Rewind it. Did you see his foot? Look how his foot is.' I mean, it'd take 10 minutes to go over one play. 'Hold on. How's he wearing his wristband? Where's his wristband at?'"

With Gill, it was always all about getting bigger, stronger, fitter, faster—things that would look good on his NBA resume.

He wasn't into bar-hopping or junk food or lounging around on the couch.

"Kendall had a dream, and he was always chasing that dream," former teammate Lowell Hamilton said. "He was determined to make that dream a reality. He didn't mix with anybody that was questionable in character or anybody that would get him off his program. He didn't drink, he didn't party, he didn't do anything.

"He was the ultimate example of the perfect athlete."

He arrived in Champaign in 1986 with a waif's waist, linguini for legs and a shaky shot.

John Dixon, The News-Gazette

NOT ONLY COULD KENDALL GILL SCORE AND PLAY DEFENSE, HE ALSO HAD
A SOFT TOUCH FROM THE FREE THROW LINE. GILL'S 13-FOR-13 EFFORT
AGAINST MINNESOTA IN 1990 RANKS THIRD BEST IN ILLINOIS HISTORY.

"And nerdy," said Hamilton, who took Gill around on his official visit. "He was very nerdy."

He wasn't Mr. Basketball like Nick Anderson. He wasn't News-Gazette Player of the Year like Larry Smith. He wasn't a McDonald's All-American like Hamilton and Marcus Liberty.

"I wasn't the most highly sought-after recruit they had, by any stretch of the imagination," Gill said. "I can remember coming into the Varsity Room for media day right before my freshman year, and nobody even knew who I was. I just sat in the corner and watched Nick and Steve (Bardo) and Larry Smith and those guys get the accolades. My hometown newspaper didn't even come up to me."

He left four years later with a body by Jake, a Big Ten scoring title and a high-paying job.

He's now a starter in the NBA, with millions stashed away and a house so big, it ought to have a moat around it.

Goes to show what a little extra time in the weight room can do.

"In life, I've always been the one that's had to prove himself," Gill said. "I overcame a lot of things just by working harder than everybody."

No one went at it like Gill, the last Illini to lead the league in scoring.

No one.

"Not even Kenny Battle," Small said.

"Kendall wanted very much to be a star and worked extremely hard to get to that point," said Jimmy Collins, who recruited him and now lives down the street from him. "When he got into lifting weights, it was a religion to him. When he got into working on his jump shot, it was a religion to him. When he got into rebounding, it was a religion to him. He wanted to be the best—and he wouldn't settle for anything less."

To help him get there, Gill enlisted the help of Jim Anderson, the head of Illinois' Educational Policy Studies department and the Jack Lalanne of Campustown.

It was the summer of 1988, right before Gill was about to enter his junior year and Illinois was about to embark on its most memorable basketball season ever.

Anderson came highly recommended by Tony Clements, director of campus recreation and a longtime official scorer at Illinois games. Anderson had helped design conditioning programs for Eddie Johnson, George Montgomery, Quinn Richardson and others in past summers, and was happy to help out Gill.

"Kendall was the one person who, the day after I talked to him about working out, was working out," Clements said.

And how.

Anderson describes their daily routine (consult your physician before trying this): "We'd go out on the football field, and he'd run a 60-yard dash at three-quarters speed, then he'd jog 40. Then he'd turn around and run 60 and jog 40. We'd start at 20 and then add one each day until he got to 40. And then when he got to 40, he'd drop back to 20 and run them at 100 percent speed."

Makes you tired just reading it.

"Not only would it put you in great condition, but also it made a basketball court seem very small," Anderson said. "When you're used to running 60-yard dashes, a basketball court is like nothing."

By the end of the summer, Gill was a regular Bruce Jenner.

"He was kind of in his own driven, motivated world," P.J. Bowman said. "We all liked Kendall, but he was kind of a loner. He had a different level of desire of trying to reach personal goals."

The next season was Gill's big breakthrough. He always was dynamite on defense— "Kendall Gill, who couldn't he defend?" former Iowa coach Tom Davis said—but hadn't been too sharp a shot, connecting on 21.1 percent of his three-pointers in Big Ten action as a sophomore.

His shot also came around in the summer of '88, Gill hoisting 300 or so a day. Fans got a glimpse of the new and improved Gill at July's Prairie State Games, when he shot like John Wayne.

"That summer, I worked as hard as I've ever worked," he said. "When I came in, I was ready. I didn't fear anything. I felt like I was right there among the top two players on the team at that time."

He came back to campus 12 pounds heavier, Barkley-confident and determined never to let a bunch of Hawkeye hecklers get to him like they did the year before in a 2-for-10 nightmare at Iowa.

"The most improved player I've ever seen," Hamilton said.

He led the team in three-pointers and was named an honorable mention All-American. This, despite missing 12 games with a stress fracture he suffered in January, when Illinois was 17-0 and ranked No. 1 in the nation.

Had Gill not gone down, former Michigan coach Bill Frieder said the Illini might not have lost.

The whole season.

"It's interesting," coach Lou Henson said. "You know, we didn't lose a game when Kendall Gill was in the lineup until Michigan beat us in the Final Four."

A DISHEARTENING LOSS TO DAYTON TURNED OUT TO BE **MARCUS LIBERTY'S** FINAL GAME AS AN **ILLINI. LIBERTY,** WHO LEFT SCHOOL AFTER HIS JUNIOR YEAR, WAS ONE OF THREE **ILLINI** TAKEN IN THE **1990** DRAFT.

Dayton Disaster

MARCH 15, 1990
BY LOREN TATE
NEWS-GAZETTE SPORTS EDITOR

AUSTIN, Tex.—The NCAA upset bug snipped fruitlessly at favored Oklahoma, North Carolina and Arkansas here Thursday.

Then it took a huge bite out of uninspired Illinois just before midnight.

Raided for 15 steals by hustling, pressing Dayton, the Illini found themselves fighting from an 11-point deficit. And, despite 28-point heroics by All-American Kendall Gill, they fell back into their pre-1989 tournament doldrums.

Dayton won 88-86, Gill's fifth three-pointer tightening the score with three seconds left, too late to save it.

It was Illinois' first loss to a non-Big Ten opponent in 28 games, dating to an NCAA fadeout against Villanova in 1988.

"We were never able to regain the emotion we had in our last two Big Ten games against Iowa and Indiana," UI coach Lou Henson said. "We have deficiencies, and we aren't good enough to win away from home without emotion. Most of the top teams didn't play real well today—that often happens in the first round—and they'll all probably be sharper Saturday.

"I think we'd have been sharper Saturday too, except we won't be playing."

The shaky, uncertain effort was mindful of tournaments past. Except for the Final Four run in 1989, when the Illini won four of five tournament games, they stand 7-8 in NCAA activity since making their first NCAA appearance in 18 years in 1981.

The Illini (21-8) shot 43.5 percent from the field and were 6 of 21 on three-pointers. Illinois, the Big Ten leader in turnover margin, showed a minus eight in the ball handling department, thus failing to take advantage of Ervin Small's 14 rebounds in a 50-40 backboard edge.

"I don't want to take anything away from Dayton, but that wasn't a pretty game," Henson said. "Neither team played well. There were two or three times this season when we didn't handle the press well, and this was one of them. This team has to execute to win, and we didn't execute."

John Dixon, The News-Gazette

DEON THOMAS, WITH ATTORNEY STEVEN
BECKETT, WAS THE FOCAL POINT OF AN INVESTIGA-
TION LAUNCHED BY THE NCAA. THE SANCTIONS IN-
CLUDED A ONE-YEAR BAN FROM POSTSEASON PLAY.

A Dark Day

NOVEMBER 6, 1990
BY BOB ASMUSSEN
NEWS-GAZETTE STAFF WRITER

O VERLAND PARK, Kan.—Not guilty and innocent are not the same, at least according to the NCAA enforcement staff.

The NCAA placed the Illinois men's basketball program on three-year probation Wednesday, including a one-year ban on postseason play and a two-year reduction of scholarships.

The 16-month investigation didn't find the Illini program guilty of any major charges in the original Official Inquiry. The sanctions were imposed because of three illegal contact violations, six self-reported violations and a lack of institutional control.

S. David Berst, NCAA assistant executive director in charge of enforcement, said: "The question has been, 'Would we allege the same things if we were to start over again and do the case?' And the answer is yes."

The original basis for the NCAA investigation—that the university made cash payments to recruits Deon Thomas and LaPhonso Ellis—was not part of the final verdict.

The investigation was the third involving the UI in the last six years. Because of its status as a repeat offender, the UI basketball program could have been given the so-called "death penalty," which includes shutting down a program for up to two seasons.

"This committee did not feel the nature of the violations warranted a reduction in regular season games," NCAA director of enforcement Chuck Smrt said.

Illinois officials said they likely will not appeal the penalties. Chancellor Morton Weir, athletic director John Mackovic and basketball coach Lou Henson said they were disappointed by the NCAA's finding that the university failed to exercise control over its basketball program.

"The lack of control (charge) bothers me," Henson said. "The university, in my opinion, they've taken drastic steps to control athletics."

The sanction guarantees the end of the UI's eight-year streak of appearances in the NCAA tournament.

LARRY SMITH'S TWO FREE THROWS CAPPED
AN ILLINOIS WIN AT IOWA THAT SAW LOU HENSON
AND IOWA'S TOM DAVIS SHAKE HANDS. HENSON
HAD AVOIDED DAVIS IN A PREVIOUS MEETING.

Payback Time

FEBRUARY 23, 1991
BY LOREN TATE
NEWS-GAZETTE SPORTS EDITOR

IOWA CITY, Iowa—Streak-shooting Andy Kaufmann had a good feeling Saturday night.

"I was licking my chops," he said. "In this kind of game, I can do a lot of damage."

Kaufmann scored a game-high 32 points as Illinois beat Iowa 79-74 in Deon Thomas' first trip to Carver-Hawkeye Arena at the conclusion of a long NCAA investigation.

A pregame meeting of Illinois coach Lou Henson and Iowa coach Tom Davis was watched closely. Henson, who refused to shake Davis' hand before or after the 53-50 Illini win in Champaign, shook it Saturday. Henson carefully avoided Iowa assistant Bruce Pearl, who turned in the Illini for ultimately rejected violations in the recruitment of Thomas.

"I thought about it a great deal," Henson said. "Only the head coach understands a lot of the things that happened. But I decided not to (avoid Davis) again."

Thomas, who did not start, made 5 of 6 shots and scored 12 points. Iowa fans booed him and waved car keys at him, but he didn't seem to mind.

"This was a team win, not a personal grudge," Thomas said. "The fans really weren't as bad as I expected. I didn't hear much of what they said in the second half."

Iowa junior James Moses said he appreciated the fans' booing the Illini "because the Illinois fans were very rude to us in Champaign . . . and the players really have no knowledge of that controversy."

Running free through a strung-out Iowa defense, Kaufmann went on a 9-for-10 binge after halftime as the Illini weathered Iowa's customary rally in the last eight minutes. Moses scored 20 of his team-high 30 points in the last seven minutes to pull Iowa within 76-74.

Rennie Clemons' steal and Larry Smith's two free throws with five seconds left sealed the win.

"We were trying to cover the arc at the end, and we were doing everything we could to stop Moses, but he was super," Henson said.

DEON THOMAS

PERSEVERANCE PLUS

BY JEFF D'ALESSIO

He came to Illinois in 1989 with his own attorney, a tarnished reputation and NCAA investigators on his case.

He left five years later with a bunch of school records, a bachelor's degree and a professional future awaiting him overseas.

In the end, things worked out all right for Deon Thomas, who overcame double teams and bogus recruiting charges to become one of Illinois' all-time greats.

"People should remember Deon as a young man who went through some very, very heavy adversity, went through some trying times, overcame some lies and ended up being the leading scorer in the history of Illinois," said former Illinois assistant Jimmy Collins, who brought him to campus.

He's still Illinois' all-time leader in points (2,129), blocked shots (177), field goals (803) and loyalty (lots).

That's what Thomas hopes fans remember him for—how he stayed true to his school. It was tough to do in the fall of 1989, when NCAA officials were grilling him about a secretly taped telephone conversation the year before between him and Iowa assistant Bruce Pearl. On the tape, Pearl asked Thomas, one of the most highly recruited high school players in America, what he thought about Illinois offering him a Chevrolet and $80,000 to come to Champaign.

Thomas realizes now he should have hung up on the guy, but being a kid, he played along with Pearl without actually denying the allegation. The charge was later thrown out by the NCAA, but it was the impetus for a long investigation that ultimately led to probation.

"I had chances to desert the university when I was going through all that trouble," Thomas said. "The NCAA told me, 'If you leave Illinois, we'll drop the investigation.' I thought about it, but the bottom line was that Illinois was the place I wanted to be and it's where my grandmother wanted me to be. So I decided to stick it out."

Illinois fans are happy he did. After being held out his first year and scoring 452 points his second, Thomas went on to win back-to-back-to-back Illini MVP awards.

He got rooked out of All-Big Ten honors, but is All-Illini all-time all the way. The only player in school history to top the 2,000-point mark, the 6-foot-9 center also finished just seven rebounds shy of Efrem Winters' school record.

"Deon was great to work with," Lou Henson said. "In five years here, not once did he ever talk back. He's the finest offensive postman I've coached."

When Thomas was about to break Eddie Johnson's all-time scoring record as a senior, Johnson told him to go for it. That's Thomas' same advice for Cory Bradford or Brian Cook or whoever else comes along after them.

Robert K. O'Daniell, The News-Gazette

ALL-TIME ILLINOIS SCORING LEADER DEON THOMAS CARRIED ON THE SIMEON TRADITION, WEARING NO. 25 IN HONOR OF THE LATE BEN WILSON. NICK ANDERSON AND BRYANT NOTREE ALSO WORE THE NUMBER.

Thomas doesn't need it anymore.

"It's a big source of pride for me, but I expect it to be broken," he said. "Records are meant to be broken."

A second-round draft pick of the Dallas Mavericks in 1994, Thomas has spent the last six seasons starring abroad. He's been in Spain five years and Israel one, playing the 1999-2000 season in Spain's Canary Islands.

If he has it his way, he'll spend the next five seasons in Spain, then get into the real estate business back in the States.

"Life in Spain is great," he said. "Especially now that I speak Spanish."

ANDY KAUFMANN LOOKS FOR ROOM AGAINST IOWA. HE BEAT THE HAWKEYES ON A SHOT THAT RIVALS NICK ANDERSON'S, EDDIE JOHNSON'S, DEREK HARPER'S AND BOB STARNES' AS THE MOST MEMORABLE IN SCHOOL HISTORY.

Delfina Colby, The News-Gazette

The Shot, The Sequel

FEBRUARY 4, 1993
BY LOREN TATE
NEWS-GAZETTE SPORTS EDITOR

CHAMPAIGN—Irrepressible Andy Kaufmann rendered meaningless 39 minutes and 59 seconds of previous action Thursday.

The Jacksonville senior, spearing a deep sideline pass from T.J. Wheeler with 1.5 seconds on the clock, drilled a perfect three-pointer to rock ninth-ranked Iowa, 78-77, and kick off the most emotional Assembly Hall celebration in years.

"It's a dream of mine to hit a last-second shot and win a game, and it happened," said Kaufmann, putting the perfect ending to a 25-point night. "That's a designed play, and it worked to perfection."

With the score tied at 75, Iowa held for the last shot. Acie Earl's side jumper barely hit the rim, then bounced off Deon Thomas' arm and shoulder right into the hoop. The basket was credited to slender Hawkeye Jim Bartels with the accompanying note by the official statistician: "Some sort of wacky basket off the rebound."

"It was going to be a tough way for us to lose with the ball hitting off Deon's shoulder," Wheeler said.

Wheeler helped haul it out. With :01.5 on the clock, he threw deep to Kaufmann, who turned for a basket that left the Hawkeyes speechless.

"In 38 years, I've never experienced a game like that," Illinois coach Lou Henson said. "It looked like a heart-breaker after the rebound caromed off Deon for an Iowa basket. The finish was just unbelievable."

Kaufmann's game-winner was the third Illini three-pointer in the last 1:44 and the 11th of the game. That's the way Henson had planned it, attacking Iowa's defense at its most vulnerable place, the wings.

Suddenly Illinois, climbing from a six-point deficit in the last two minutes, is 6-2 and tied with Michigan for second place in the Big Ten and challenging for a top 25 berth.

Instead of trailing Iowa 57-56 in the series, the Illini have forged ahead by this single victory, and they have defeated Tom Davis and his hard-working Hawkeyes in five of the last six meetings.

Mark Cowan, The News-Gazette

BRYANT NOTREE WON THE PRAISE OF DUKE COACH MIKE KRZYZEWSKI FOR HIS EFFORTS IN THE ILLINI'S IMPROBABLE WIN IN DURHAM. IT WAS THE BLUE DEVILS' FIRST LOSS IN 96 NONCONFERENCE HOME GAMES.

· · · · · · · ·

Duking It Out

DECEMBER 2, 1995
BY LOREN TATE
NEWS-GAZETTE SPORTS EDITOR

D URHAM, N.C.—Duke's quest for the Three-I sweep of the Big Ten Conference was foiled Saturday night in a shocking upset that could rocket Illinois into the Top 25.

Mike Krzyzewski's 12th-ranked Blue Devils had extended their Big Ten streak to 16-1 with Alaska wins over Indiana and Iowa, and carried a 95-game Cameron Indoor Stadium streak against nonconference teams when suddenly, unexpectedly, Illinois turned the tables, 75-65.

"This was the biggest win by far since I've been at Illinois," junior Jerry Hester said. "For us to come in here and face this tradition and this crowd, and do what we did, is very big.

"I can't explain our free-throwing (the UI was 2 for 15 at one point). We just have to concentrate harder."

With Duke ahead 60-59 on a trey by Jeff Capel, Illini junior Kiwane Garris came to the rescue with three consecutive steals that led to two baskets and a rebound goal by Jerry Gee. Then Richard Keene swiped a Duke pass, sending Garris to the line for two tosses that made it 67-60 with 50 seconds to go.

Garris didn't start due to a strained groin muscle but played 28 minutes and was there when the Illini needed him, cashing 6 of 7 free throws for a team that was otherwise an unstrung 4 of 18 at the line.

"I thought overall that this was the toughest game we've been in," Krzyzewski said. "Illinois' offense is well-conceived and very difficult to handle. You can't play off of anybody.

"They knocked us back early. Then we got in position to win in the second half and played pretty well for 17 1/2 minutes. I thought (Bryant) Notree gave Illinois a lift off the bench. He sparked them with some big baskets at the right moments."

The 6-foot-4 sophomore played his best game, finishing off a 14-point performance with a dunk with five seconds left. Garris and Keene combined for 32 points and 11 assists although neither played more than 30 minutes.

Robin Scholz, The News-Gazette

LOU HENSON THREW EVERYONE FOR A LOOP WHEN HE
ANNOUNCED HIS RETIREMENT AFTER A WIN AGAINST IOWA.
HENSON WOULD LATER COME OUT OF RETIREMENT TO COACH
NEW MEXICO STATE TO THE NCAA TOURNAMENT.

Lou's Through

FEBRUARY 24, 1996
BY LOREN TATE
NEWS-GAZETTE SPORTS EDITOR

CHAMPAIGN—The University of Illinois' winningest basketball coach caught the sports world by surprise Saturday afternoon with a stunning announcement that he will retire after 21 seasons with the Fighting Illini.

Less than a year shy of his 65th birthday and with speculation building, Lou Henson stepped into an Assembly Hall locker room bubbling from a 91-86 defeat of Iowa, and informed the players of his decision. He then read from a written statement, formulated with wife Mary the night before, to the media.

"When it became painfully apparent that my proximity to retirement was beginning to adversely affect our recruiting plans, the decision was made to step aside," Henson said. In an aside, he noted: "To do otherwise would be selfish on my part. To stay another year would set recruiting back."

Henson lifted Illinois up among the nation's leaders in the 1980s, the UI making nine NCAA tournament appearances in 10 seasons before NCAA sanctions interrupted a working string of eight. Henson has a 422-220 audit at Illinois, and is seventh on the active Division I list of coaches with a 662-327 record in 34 seasons.

He had mulled the final decision for three weeks. In fact, when the Illini team plane lifted off over Penn State on February 8, following yet another tough setback, Henson wasn't analyzing the game or scratching away as he usually does on strategy options.

Seated next to Mary, he spent much of the two-hour flight drawing up his own personal proposal list for presentation to athletic director Ron Guenther. Henson turned over his recommendations to attorney Tom Harrington the next morning, and Harrington set up a meeting with Guenther to hammer out, in general terms, the details of Henson's retirement.

Both Henson and Guenther preferred to wait until the season had been concluded, but rumors were growing, so Henson decided Friday and told Guenther on Saturday morning that he would make his announcement directly after Saturday's game.

LOU HENSON'S 214 BIG TEN WINS
RANK FOURTH ALL-TIME BEHIND BOB
KNIGHT, GENE KEADY AND WARD LAM-
BERT. IN 21 SEASONS, HENSON WENT 214-
164 IN CONFERENCE GAMES.

Robin Scholz, The News-Gazette

LOU HENSON

LOU CAN DO

BY JEFF D'ALESSIO

Lou Henson has gotten so many questions about his 'do over the years, he devoted the first chapter of his autobiography to the matter.

Getting his due, however, hasn't been so easy.

"Henson has never really been given the kind of credit that he should have as a coach," said his old rival, Indiana's Bob Knight. "Of all the coaches in the Big Ten that have been here while I've been coaching, I don't think that anybody has had a better grasp of defensive play than he had.

"(Lon Kruger's 1997-98 Big Ten championship) team, if I'm not mistaken, almost everyone that was a contributor was one of Henson's players, was he not? They had a really good background with Henson, and I think more than anything else, that enabled Illinois to continue to do well after he left."

Only four active coaches have won more college basketball games than Henson, who entered the 2000-2001 season, his 38th at the helm, with 726. Jim Phelan of Mount St. Mary's has 809. Knight's at 763. Jerry Tarkanian has 733, one more than Lefty Driesell.

Henson's one of 11 coaches to take two different teams to the Final Four, doing it in 1989 at Illinois and 1970 at New Mexico State.

He's the all-time winningest coach at Illinois, and just 13 wins away from doing the same at New Mexico State.

And his next 20-win season will be his 20th—something only nine of his peers have pulled off.

So when's Henson going to get his bust in the Hall of Fame? That's what New Mexico State athletic director Jim Paul wants to know. Paul recently enlisted the help of the former sports information director at Texas-El Paso who launched Don Haskins' successful Hall of Fame campaign to help out with Henson. Paul plans to nominate his guy every year until he gets in.

"I don't know how they can keep Lou Henson out," Paul said.

MARY HENSON, LEFT, JOINED HER HUSBAND AT AN EMO-
TIONAL RETIREMENT NEWS CONFERENCE ON FEB. 24,
1996. TWO WEEKS LATER, HE WAS HONORED AT A LAVISH
POSTGAME CEREMONY.

State. It was a big deal in Las Cruces, N.M., where Henson's a hero.

The pride of Okay, Okla., spent almost as many years in Las Cruces as he did in Champaign-Urbana. He played college ball there from 1953-55, coached high school ball there from 1957-62, coached college ball there from 1966-75, then unexpectedly returned to coach the Aggies in the fall of 1997.

Henson had announced his retirement from coaching a year earlier, but his alma mater needed him. It was the middle of October, a few days before the start of practice, and New Mexico State had just fired its coach.

Henson, 65 at the time, agreed to give up the bridge games and golf courses and return to the sidelines on a volunteer basis for one season.

Six months. That's it.

"I wouldn't have gone anyplace else because I was enjoying retirement," he said at an October 16, 1997, ceremony. "I think I owe this institution, this community and this state something because I probably wouldn't have been in coaching if it weren't for the people here. I felt that's the least I could do: come back and serve this university for six more months."

Three years later, he's still going strong. And Paul's still making his Henson-for-the-Hall pitch to anyone who'll listen.

Only 13 men in the history of the game have won 700, and eight of them are in. It's an elite club. John Wooden didn't win 700. Neither did John Thompson. Nor John Chaney.

If Paul needs letters of recommendation, he ought to hit up Henson's old Illini assistants, who've grown a little touchy over all the criticism of their coach. Such as Henson's supposed inability to "win the big one," which he and the Flyin' Illini heard all about in March 1989 when they arrived in Minneapolis for the Sweet 16.

"I don't know what the big game is," Mark Coomes said. "Is the (1988) Missouri game—

Just two active coaches have been inducted: Knight, winner of three national championships, and Crum, winner of two. Henson's titleless, but has plenty of other glittery credentials sure to catch the eye of voters.

"Seven hundred wins and Final Fours at two different schools certainly makes you a strong candidate," said author John Feinstein, who once served on the Hall of Fame's selection committee. "I think Lefty Driesell's going to be in the Hall of Fame someday, and he's got 700 wins and no Final Fours.

"The thing that might work against Lou Henson a little bit is the probation at Illinois. The committee would take that into account, regardless of whether anybody in Champaign thinks it's fair or unfair or he was responsible or not responsible. He was running the show and the school got put on probation.

"If that had not happened, 700 wins and Final Fours at two different schools, to me, would make him a lock."

Henson joined the 700 club on February 25, 1999, with a win against Big West rival Utah

being down 17 and coming back to win by three—a big game? We beat Missouri eight straight times. Were those big games? Eight straight years. How do you classify big games? When you beat Indiana five straight times and three of them are at their place, are those big games? Who's ever done that in their lives? Who's ever beaten Indiana three straight times at Indiana?

"When we beat Purdue six straight times and three of those were overtime games and one of those was with 'Big Dog,' were those big games? When we beat the national champions two times in one year, are those big games? I don't know. Only writers define big games. And only the next game that you lose is the big game you didn't win.

"The interesting thing about his reputation is that they recognize him for his ability to recruit and not coach. I think it's the opposite. I don't think he was a top recruiter, but he was an excellent coach."

Henson should have stuck Coomes on that sportswriter in Seattle who broke down the 1989 Illinois-Michigan national semifinal position by position. He gave the frontcourt edge to Michigan. Backcourt, Illinois. Coaching, Michigan.

Steve Fisher was coaching his fifth game at Michigan. Henson was in his 28th season.

"Coach Henson gets maligned a lot, but he did a wonderful job with us," said Stephen Bardo, a Flyin' Illini guard. "People don't realize that one of the reasons teams win is because they're well-prepared. When they lose, a lot of times it's because they see something they're not used to seeing, and it's like, 'Uh-oh.' We were never surprised by anybody."

"It's true," center Lowell Hamilton said. "He had you prepared. Oh, you could lock a team down because he knew exactly what their personnel could do and when you followed his directions defensively, his predictions were right on the money. They weren't even predictions. He knew."

Robert K. O'Daniell, The News-Gazette

KENDALL GILL, RIGHT, WAS ONE OF FIVE FIRST-ROUND PICKS TO PLAY FOR LOU HENSON AT ILLINOIS, JOINING NICK ANDERSON, KENNY BATTLE, DEREK HARPER AND KEN NORMAN.

John Dixon, The News-Gazette

LOU HENSON IS THE LAST ILLINOIS COACH TO BE NAMED BIG TEN COACH OF THE YEAR, PICKING UP THE HONOR IN 1993, WHEN HIS TEAM WENT 19-13 AND ADVANCED TO THE SECOND ROUND OF THE NCAA TOURNAMENT.

JIMMY COLLINS SIGNALS TO THE CROWD BEFORE HIS FIRST GAME AS HEAD COACH AT ILLINOIS-CHICAGO. THE POPULAR FORMER ILLINI ASSISTANT LOST TO LON KRUGER'S FIRST TEAM 68-63 BEFORE A SELLOUT CROWD.

Collins vs. Kruger

NOVEMBER 22, 1996
BY JEFF D'ALESSIO
NEWS-GAZETTE STAFF WRITER

CHICAGO—Lon Kruger wasn't about to say it, so Brian Johnson said it for him. There are better ways to tip off a new era than how Kruger's first University of Illinois men's basketball team went about it Friday night.

"You win, and people say you were supposed to," UI forward Johnson said. "You lose, and the wheels fell off and everyone's upset."

The Illini didn't let the pressures of playing against their former coach (Jimmy Collins) in a hostile atmosphere (UIC Pavilion) against a team they were supposed to smack silly (Illinois-Chicago) bug them too much, beating the Flames 68-63 in Kruger's debut.

"Now we can go on with our careers and the rest of our lives," said UI forward Bryant Notree, glad to put it behind him.

With Notree and the rest of the bench off (3 for 18) and a loud, pro-Collins crowd of 8,715 pushing their Flames higher, the Illini turned to seniors Kiwane Garris and Jerry Hester to win their fifth straight season opener.

Kruger expected the emotional roller coaster, what with the first sellout in UIC history, the tight history of the series and Collins on the other side of the scorer's table.

He said he kind of enjoyed the atmosphere, the circumstances, the pressure.

"Most openers are probably not this emotional," Kruger said. "But any time you can play in an atmosphere like this and come out with a win, it's good. We'll learn from this."

After the final buzzer, Collins stood still as the players he used to watch over smothered him with handshakes and hugs.

"I'd rather it be me going to hug them (after a win)," Collins said. "It doesn't ease the pain. Winning always feels better than losing."

Collins, passed over during last spring's search for Lou Henson's replacement, was asked the difference between being an assistant and a head coach.

"The headaches," he said.

KIWANE GARRIS

PEAK PERFORMER

BY JEFF D'ALESSIO

As his career was coming to a close, Kiwane Garris was asked what one moment he'd remember most from his days as an Illini.

Would it be his MVP performance at the 1994 San Juan Shootout? Becoming the first freshman in Big Ten history to score 30 points in back-to-back games? Helping put an end to Duke's 95-game nonconference homecourt winning streak as a junior?

Nope. None of the above. Instead of a highlight, the UI's two-time All-Big Ten point guard chose a low one: a 108-107 triple-overtime loss to Missouri in 1993. Garris missed two free throws at the end of the second overtime that night, bringing half the St. Louis Arena to near tears.

The only time he felt worse was a few weeks later when a heavy package arrived for him at the Illinois basketball office with a Columbia, Mo., postmark.

Its contents: two bricks.

"That really motivated me, made me play harder, made me play good against them," Garris said.

From that day forward, Garris vowed he'd never let his team down at the end of the game again.

He kept his word.

Garris went on to sink 615 free throws, most in school history. He became one of college basketball's coolest customers when the clock was winding down and the game was on the line, putting away team after team with his free throw shooting.

"I love to take on a challenge," Garris said. "It's fun to me."

Thirty seconds left, Illinois up one?

Bring it on.

"You can't ever feel comfortable in a close game at the end, but with him out there you always felt like the game's in pretty good hands," former Illini Ted Beach said.

Those hands hit a school-record 17 of 17 against Cal in 1996, a school-record 39 in a row during one sophomore stretch and a school-record 245 as a senior.

"The last two minutes were what I like to call Kiwane time," former Illini Doug Altenberger said. "He knows that. The other team knows that. He gets the ball and makes them do what they don't want to do, which is foul him, and he makes the free throws.

"His whole career, if Illinois had the lead and they got the ball in Kiwane's hands, 99 percent of the time they came away with a 'W.' Steve Alford was the same way at Indiana. They just take over at the end and win the game."

That's just one of the reasons Altenberger thinks Garris is the greatest Illinois point guard of them all.

Better than Derek Harper. Better than Bruce Douglas. Better than Stephen Bardo, Frank Williams, any of them.

Teak Phillips, The News-Gazette

KIWANE GARRIS' DREAM CAME TRUE IN 1997, WHEN THE ILLINOIS SENIOR WON HIS FIRST NCAA TOURNAMENT GAME. ILLINOIS BEAT SOUTHERN CAL 90-77 IN CHARLOTTE, N.C.

"Derek, offensively, was not nearly as good as Kiwane is. Derek was a little bit more physically bigger and stronger, but fundamentally, I don't think there's been anybody better than Kiwane," Altenberger said. "Derek was a great defensive player, Douglas was a great assist man and Bardo was Mr. Consistency.

"But if you were to grade out all those guys, Kiwane would be the best point guard Illinois has ever had. He's the complete package."

Garris didn't win as often as some of the elite point guards in Illini history (just one

NCAA victory), but his resume could match anyone's.

Only Deon Thomas scored more points than Garris at Illinois. Only Douglas had more assists. Only Richard Keene sank more three-pointers.

And no one was named to more All-Big Ten teams, bagged more Illinois MVP awards or hit more free throws.

"If he's not one of the best perimeter players ever there, I'd like to see the best," former UI assistant Jimmy Collins said.

John Dixon, The News-Gazette

THE ILLINOIS BENCH ERUPTS NEAR THE END OF A
21-POINT WIN OVER MATEEN CLEAVES AND MICHI-
GAN STATE. THE TEAMS WOULD FINISH THE SEA-
SON TIED FOR THE BIG TEN TITLE.

Turn Back the Clock

FEBRUARY 12, 1998
BY JEFF D'ALESSIO
NEWS-GAZETTE STAFF WRITER

CHAMPAIGN—For one night, it was 1989 all over again at the Assembly Hall. Full house. First place in the Big Ten on the line. Students storming the court. "That's what's supposed to happen when a crowd gets behind a team and a team plays with a lot of energy," Michigan State coach Tom Izzo said when one of the most memorable nights in recent Illinois basketball history was over. "It was a fun team to watch. Unfortunately, I had to watch it from the opposing bench."

Happy days are here again for the Illini, who treated a sellout crowd of 16,450 to what coach Lon Kruger called the top performance of the year, an 84-63 Thursday night whipping of Michigan State's 13th-ranked, league-leading Spartans.

"There's only one word for tonight," Illinois forward Victor Chukwudebe said. "Unbelievable."

The margin.

The fact that the Illini are now tied with the Spartans atop the Big Ten.

The noise.

You would have thought President Clinton was here or something.

"From the time we came out in warmups till the time when they ran out on the floor at the end of the game, it was a very exciting place," Illinois forward Jerry Hester said. "Whoever didn't come to the game probably heard the crowd."

Y'all come back now, ya hear?

The fans get to enjoy this one longer than the 18-7, 10-2 Illini, who head to West Lafayette, Ind., with a seven-game winning streak, half of the Big Ten lead and games left against Purdue, Northwestern, Iowa and Indiana.

That's right, Big Ten lead.

"You look up at the top of the standings and see Illinois there, it's just an unbelievable feeling," Illinois guard Kevin Turner said, repeating the word of the day. "I've never been in this position before."

BOB KNIGHT DIDN'T HAVE MANY GOOD
THINGS TO SAY ABOUT REFEREE TED VAL-
ENTINE AFTER HIS TEAM'S LOSS TO ILLINOIS.
KNIGHT WAS EJECTED FROM THE GAME,
WHICH ILLINOIS WON TO KEEP ITS BIG TEN
TITLE HOPES ALIVE.

Robert K. O'Daniell, The News-Gazette

Oh, What a Knight

FEBRUARY 24, 1998
BY JEFF D'ALESSIO
NEWS-GAZETTE STAFF WRITER

BLOOMINGTON, Ind.—After sending their coach off the deep end, making their fans' blood boil and wrecking their Senior Day, Illinois said something that really set Indiana's Hoosiers off.

Go Purdue!

"We're going to be big-time Purdue fans this weekend," Illinois senior guard Kevin Turner said. "It'd be great way to go out, as co-champions in the Big Ten."

Lost amid the hubbub surrounding Bob Knight's three-technical tizzy before a national television audience Tuesday night was this: With its 82-72 rump-kicking of Indiana, all that stands between Lon Kruger's Illini and a piece of their first Big Ten championship in 14 years is a Purdue win Saturday at Michigan State.

"I've got to talk to Rod Cardinal and find out how to cheer for Purdue," Illinois senior forward Brian Johnson said. "I'm not good at that."

Tuesday's wild win capped off the Illini's most successful Big Ten regular season since Kenny Battle & Co. took a trip to Seattle in 1989.

At worst, they have second place all to themselves. They've won 10 of their last 11 heading into the inaugural Big Ten tournament. And that makes two in a row in the House That Bobby Built, three in a row over the hated Hoosiers.

"Our guys feel good about what they've done," Kruger said. "They like what they've done. They'll cherish it for a lifetime, actually."

Knight's longtime feud with referee Ted Valentine simmered in the first half, then erupted with 9:37 left in the game, Knight getting tossed after a confusing and heated sequence underneath the Indiana basket.

"You're about to go out in life, and I'll tell you one thing," Knight said to an all-ears Assembly Hall crowd who stuck around for Senior Night activities. "You saw something here tonight that's a great indication that life isn't fair.

"I've been in basketball for 33 years as a head coach, and this tonight is the greatest travesty that I've ever seen."

Robin Scholz, The News-Gazette

JERRY HESTER SHOWS OFF THE BIG TEN CHAMPIONSHIP TROPHY, DELIVERED TO THE ILLINI BY COMMISSIONER JIM DELANY. HESTER WAS ONE OF FIVE SENIOR STARTERS ON LON KRUGER'S SECOND NCAA TEAM.

A Happy Ending

MARCH 1, 1998
BY JEFF D'ALESSIO
NEWS-GAZETTE STAFF WRITER

CHAMPAIGN—To celebrate their magic moment Sunday night, Lon Kruger's Big Ten co-champs all piled in the car and headed over to Outback Steakhouse, where dinner was on Coach.

What'll ya have, Jarrod Gee?

"I'm going to order a nice, big, juicy championship steak," the Illinois center said.

Probably better for his health than Sunday's Michigan State-Purdue heartstopper, which nearly gave the Illini and all their fans coronaries.

Illinois, needing a Boilermaker upset to grab a share of its first Big Ten championship in 14 years, got it, 99-96. But not before a crazy second half, an overtime and a Mateen Cleaves last-second halfcourt heave that just missed.

When it did, all heck broke loose at the Kruger house, where the team took in the game. The riot was captured on film by Illinois officials, who gave copies of the videotape to local TV stations.

"Everybody was going crazy," senior Kevin Turner said. "We were jumping on each other on the floor."

Then out came the boxes of hats and shirts, emblazoned with "1998 Big Ten basketball champions."

"This hat's not coming off all week," senior Jerry Hester said.

"The players have talked about getting fingers fitted for rings," Kruger said.

"Size me up," senior Brian Johnson said.

Sometime between now and next year's opener, there will also be a banner to design, like the one the Spartans put up prior to tip-off Sunday. That's an expense the Illinois athletic department may not have had in its basketball budget.

Not the men's one, anyway.

"It's something that if I told you or you told me at the beginning of the year, we both would have looked at each other like we were crazy," Johnson said.

Most publications plugged them for seventh or eighth in the Big Ten.

"No one expected us to be here," Turner said. "But we really stuck together, kept our heads up and bought into what Coach was telling us to do."

Robert K. O'Daniell, The News-Gazette

LON KRUGER HAD HIS LAST-PLACE ILLINI READY FOR THE
BIG TEN TOURNAMENT, WHERE THEY KNOCKED OFF THREE
RANKED OPPONENTS IN THREE DAYS TO REACH THE CHAMPION-
SHIP GAME. KRUGER WENT 81-48 IN FOUR SEASONS BEFORE
LEAVING FOR THE NBA.

Memorable March

MARCH 6, 1999
BY JEFF D'ALESSIO
NEWS-GAZETTE STAFF WRITER

CHICAGO—Up until just a few days ago, it'd been a historic Illinois basketball season for all the wrong reasons.

First to worst in the Big Ten standings. Most league losses in school history. Crummiest start to a conference season in 92 years.

Today, Lon Kruger's pooped Illini have a chance to make the kind of history they can be proud of.

They're a fourth upset in four days away from becoming the first team from a major conference to go from last place to win its league tournament and the automatic ticket to the NCAAs that goes with it.

"They're sitting in the locker room a week ago looking at a very abysmal season," Ohio State coach Jim O'Brien said. "And now they're looking at one win from the tournament. They've put themselves in a great position."

Can you even believe it?

"Do you believe it?" Illinois center Fess Hawkins shot back.

The 11th-seeded Illini (14-17) made believers out of a national television audience and a United Center crowd of 20,695 Saturday with their 79-77 thriller against O'Brien's 11th-ranked Buckeyes.

It was their third Big Ten tournament stunner in less than 72 hours and puts them in today's final against second-ranked, winner-of-17-straight, No. 1-NCAA-seed-to-be Michigan State.

"I think even my parents would have actually laughed at me if I said we were going to be playing in the championship game," Illinois freshman Damir Krupalija said.

O'Brien admitted he'll pull for the Illini, who'll try to become the first major conference team to go dancing with a losing record since Missouri in 1978.

"In my mind, they are unquestionably the best last-place team in America," O'Brien said.

"After this is over, wherever we finish, people can't call us losers," Sergio McClain said.

MATT HELDMAN

1976-1999

BY JEFF D'ALESSIO

Not only do they remember Matt Heldman as a good friend, a good leader and a good guard.

The Illinois basketball family also misses him for his good sense of humor.

"He didn't mind jokes played on him, and he loved playing them on other people," trainer Rod Cardinal said. "I remember my favorite one. There was a heavy metal rock group that came to the Assembly Hall sometime during Matt's tenure here, and Matt was a huge fan of them. This is before they made the renovations to the Assembly Hall, so the band used our locker room.

"The day after the concert, B.J. (Brian Johnson) and I put a note on Matt's locker, pretending we were from the band, saying, 'Gee, Matt, thanks for all your support.' We could barely keep a straight face. But Matt believed it was sincere for a couple of weeks. He'd walk around, saying, 'Can you believe they left a note in my locker?'"

You can be sure Heldman got them back a few days later.

No. 21 always had the last laugh.

He arrived in Champaign in August 1994 a gullible guard with a funny-looking crew cut, a 6-foot frame and a lot of doubters.

He left four years later with a Big Ten championship ring, a spot in the Illinois record books and a C Section full of fans.

"He was one of those self-made guys," Northwestern coach Kevin O'Neill said. "They said he was too small, too slow, too this, too that. But he was a winner."

Heldman was killed on October 10, 1999, in a two-car accident in his hometown of Libertyville. Four people died in the head-on wreck, including Heldman's basketball-loving father, Otis, who rarely missed a game his son played.

"Every time you'd go on the road and look up in the stands, he was there," said former UI assistant Dick Nagy, who recruited Heldman. "These two were inseparable. Even in death."

When former teammate Kevin Turner heard the tragic news, he immediately thought back to that magical 1997-98 season, when Lon Kruger's Illini, picked by everybody to do nothing, won a share of the Big Ten title.

Heldman was the point guard of that beloved bunch, getting the job after BYU transfer Robbie Reid turned it down. Many wondered if Heldman, a shooting guard the season before, could handle it.

"That pushed Matt even more," said Turner, who shared a backcourt with him. "Matt loved challenges."

Heldman was a hit from the start. He went 14 for 14 from the line in a December upset of Clemson. He had 19 points in a win at No. 11 Iowa two weeks later. He took Reid to school on Super Bowl Sunday.

"We had a question about who was going to be our point guard," former Illinois assistant Mike Shepherd said. "Then there was never any question who was going to be our point guard."

Heldman was an important piece to the championship puzzle, leading the team in assists, free throw percentage and three-pointers. He canned 67 threes as a senior, the eighth-best single-season total in school history.

"Great shooter," Purdue coach Gene Keady said. "Great competitor."

Before leaving for a professional stint in Finland the fall before he died, Heldman played

POPULAR POINT GUARD MATT HELDMAN SHARED THE 1996 KENNY BATTLE AWARD WITH BRYANT NOTREE. HIS HUSTLE WON OVER FANS FROM THE TIME HE STEPPED ON CAMPUS.

point guard for Athletes in Action, a Christian traveling team.

He was only on the team for a few weeks, but he left a lasting impression.

"He was as coachable a player that's ever played for us," AIA general manager Sharm Scheuerman said. "So polite, so considerate."

So missed. By teammates, by coaches, by AIA team discipler Dave Bratton, an Illinois grad who grew close to Heldman during their short time together.

"I'm confident I'm going to see him again sometime," Bratton said. "It will be a great Illini reunion."

SERGIO McCLAIN DRIVES PAST
INDIANA'S JEFFREY NEWTON IN THE ILLINI'S
FINAL HOME GAME OF 1999-2000. IT WAS
ONE OF SIX WINS IN EIGHT TRIES BY LON
KRUGER AGAINST INDIANA.

Hoosier Daddy

FEBRUARY 22, 2000
BY JEFF D'ALESSIO
NEWS-GAZETTE STAFF WRITER

CHAMPAIGN—The atmosphere was straight out of '89. Threes were going in like layups. ESPN was in town, Cory Bradford was doing his best Nick Anderson and Illinois was on its way to its biggest win against Indiana in 44 years.

Can't get any better than Tuesday's scene at the Assembly Hall.

"Yeah, it can," Illinois guard Frank Williams said. "It can get a whole lot better."

Illinois can go to Ohio State on Sunday, beat the sixth-ranked Buckeyes on CBS, climb back into the polls, take care of Northwestern and head to the Big Ten tournament in two weeks on a nine-game roll.

"A win on Sunday would rank up there with this one," UI forward Lucas Johnson said. "We're really looking forward to getting after Ohio State, but I think we're going to relish this victory for a while."

He and 16,450 hoarse fans, who couldn't believe what they were seeing Tuesday. From Bradford's shooting (sweet) to Bob Knight's mood (sour), just about everything went right for Illinois in its 87-63 rump-kicking of the 16th-ranked Hoosiers on ESPN's Super Tuesday.

"We fed off the crowd, and the crowd fed off us," UI forward Sergio McClain said.

The win was Illinois' seventh in a row and ninth in 10 tries but its first against a Top 25 team since Jan. 6, when Ohio State came to town. The Illini (18-7, 10-4 Big Ten) hit a rough spell after that, losing four of their next six before going on a six-game tear against a bunch of bottom-tier Big Ten teams.

For those wondering if they could cut it against a top-notch outfit like Indiana, you have your answer.

"I think people had their doubts about how good we really were after not playing any ranked teams in that stretch," Johnson said. "But after this one, we proved that we can hang with them and beat 'em."

Lon Kruger called it Illinois' best performance of the season.

"We had a lot of fun out there tonight," forward Damir Krupalija said.

ON JUNE 9, 2000, TULSA'S **BILL SELF** WAS INTRODUCED AS ILLINOIS' 15TH MEN'S BASKETBALL COACH. SELF REPLACED LON KRUGER, WHO LEFT UNEXPECTEDLY FOR THE ATLANTA HAWKS FOR $2 MILLION A YEAR.

John Dixon, The News-Gazette